How Analysts Think and Why

They Think the Way They Do

How Analysts Think and Why

They Think the Way They Do

Reflections on
Three Psychoanalytic Hours

Edited by

Arden Aibel Rothstein, Ph.D.
and
Samuel Abrams, M.D.

INTERNATIONAL UNIVERSITIES PRESS, INC.
Madison   Connecticut

How analysts think, and why they think the way they do : reflections on three psychoanalytic hours / edited by Arden Aibel Rothstein and Samuel Abrams.
    p. cm.
    Includes bibliographical references and index.
    ISBN 0-8236-2358-0
    1. Psychoanalysis. 2. Psychoanalytic interpretation. I. Rothstein, Arden. II. Abrams, Samuel, M.D.

    RC504.H69 2005
    616.89'17—dc21

                        2003049926

Manufactured in the United States of America

Table of Contents

Contributors

PANELISTS

M. Nasir Ilahi, L.L.M., Faculty, NYU Psychoanalytic Institute and Clinical Assistant Professor of Psychiatry,
New York University Medical Center; Visiting Lecturer, New York Psychoanalytic Institute; graduate
and member of the British Psychoanalytic Society;
member, International Psychoanalytic Association;
private practice in New York City and Greenwich,
Connecticut; author and lecturer on clinical psychoanalysis with a focus on primitive mental states and
cross-cultural issues.

Claudia Lament, Ph.D., Faculty, NYU Psychoanalytic Insti-
tute and Clinical Assistant Professor of Psychiatry,
New York University Medical Center; graduate of
NYU Psychoanalytic Institute and the Anna Freud
Centre, London (qualified child and adolescent psy-
choanalyst); author of several psychoanalytic papers,
most recently "The Consultation Process with an
Adult: A Child Analyst's Perspective," *Journal of the
American Psychoanalytic Association* and "Technical Is-
sues in Adolescent Analysis: A Jamesian View," *The
Psychoanalytic Study of the Child.*

Kathleen Lyon, M.D., Faculty, NYU Psychoanalytic Institute
and Clinical Assistant Professor of Psychiatry, New
York University Medical Center; graduate of NYU Psychoanalytic Institute; author, "Shattered Mirror: A
Fragment of a Treatment of a Patient with Multiple
Personality Disorder," *Psychoanalytic Inquiry*; full-
time private practice in Manhattan.

Peter B. Neubauer, M.D., Faculty, Training Analyst Emeritus and current Supervisor in Child Psychoanalysis, NYU Psychoanalytic Institute Clinical Professor of Psychiatry, New York University Medical Center; Editor, *The Psychoanalytic Study of the Child*; Past President, Association for Child Psychoanalysis; author, *Process of Child Development and Nature's Thumbprint,* among others; Former Director, Child Development Center, New York City; practice of child and adult analysis in New York City.

Shelley Orgel, M.D., Faculty, Supervising and Training Analyst, and former Director, NYU Psychoanalytic Institute, Clinical Professor of Psychiatry, New York University Medical Center; Associate Editor, *The Psychoanalytic Quarterly*; Past Chairman, Board of Professional Standards, American Psychoanalytic Association; author of papers on many psychoanalytic subjects: time, Medea and gifts, Iago, Chekhov, Henry Adams, Sylvia Plath, suicide, "Freud and Femininity" (Freud Lecture of Psychoanalytic Association of New York), termination of analysis (American Psychoanalytic Association Plenary Lecture), and hazards to neutrality in training analysis (Brill Memorial Lecture, New York Psychoanalytic Society and in press, *The Psychoanalytic Quarterly*).

EDITORS

Samuel Abrams, M.D., Faculty, Supervising and Training Analyst and former Director, NYU Psychoanalytic Institute; Clinical Professor of Psychiatry, New York University Medical Center; Editor, *The Psychoanalytic Study of the Child* and Editorial Board, *The Psychoanalytic Quarterly*; author of more than sixty published papers on psychoanalysis.

Arden Aibel Rothstein, Ph.D., Faculty, Supervising and Training Analyst, NYU Psychoanalytic Institute; Clinical Professor of Psychiatry, New York University Medical Center; author of psychoanalytic papers on varied subjects and coauthor of two books: A. A. Rothstein and J. Glenn, *Learning Disabilities and Psychic Conflict: A Psychoanalytic Casebook* and A. Rothstein, L. Benjamin, M. Crosby, and K. Eisenstadt, *Learning Disorders: An Integration of Neuropsychological and Psychoanalytic Considerations.*

Preface: The Volume's Historical Context

This volume is not only a scientific contribution but an historical one as well, illustrating the work-in-progress trends of one institute, NYU Psychoanalytic Institute at New York University Medical Center. Twenty-five years ago members of the same institute published several collections of articles regarded as testaments to its vigor and to beliefs in its then fundamental orienting perspectives. The resulting volumes illustrated group coherence and firmly shared beliefs. The perspectives proposed by the contributing analysts served the clinical illustrations that were offered, reflected the theories that were honored, and seemed eminently useful, even for the papers on "applied" psychoanalysis that filled many of these volumes.

Now on the occasion of its fiftieth anniversary as a functioning affiliate of the American Psychoanalytic Association, the current volume illustrates a discipline in flux. It concentrates on the clinical, it embodies the readiness of faculty members to challenge one another, and it inquires about the dangers of thinking in an excessively assertive and self-satisfied manner. Most significantly, there is a greater willingness to accept how much is not known.

One of the vehicles for the fiftieth anniversary celebration was an all-day symposium comprised of two related panels. The morning panel addressed how theoretical perspectives inform clinical data while the afternoon panel addressed how training informs clinical perspectives. The morning panel, which is the nidus of this volume (see our Introduction for further elaboration) was particularly stimulating because of its focus upon clinical matters.

In a brief introduction, the chair, Dr. Howard Welsh, noted that an anniversary affords the opportunity for taking stock of growth and change. It was his impression that there were considerable differences between the form and content of contemporary presentations from those that existed fifty years before, when the Institute was born, and even twenty-five years earlier when the Institute celebrated its first quarter century of growth. Of those differences, Dr. Welsh particularly cited the increased attention to subjectivity in the clinical setting, a notion that might not have been so highly regarded many years earlier. He expressed the view that contemporary analysts are more inclined to be aware of their own subjectivity, are more open to describing their experiences in clinical seminars, and to use self-awareness in their search for other forms of therapeutic action.

Although Dr. Welsh's interest in a historical perspective was put aside that morning in favor of the focus upon clinical issues, there is evidence to support his impression of important changes. Fifty years earlier, when the Institute first appeared, its predominant organizing center was Sigmund Freud. In-depth knowledge of Freud—his thinking and even the events in his life—was regarded as an essential requirement in the education of analysts. Theory was taught in historical sequence, recapitulating how Freud thought about his cases and why he thought the way he did. Oedipality and sexuality were basic dynamic ingredients. Metapsychology, a newly conceived term, was seen by many as a necessary base to organize theories at different levels of abstraction. The word *developmental* had only just begun to be used by child analysts, originally within a context to distinguish it from *maturational,* although training in child analysis at the Institute was still only a future prospect. Resolution of the infantile neurosis was celebrated as the center of therapeutic action. "Objectivity," and the intrapsychic—what would now be called one-person psychology—were the fashion.

Twenty-five years later, the Institute marked a seminal anniversary by publishing a series of four volumes. Continuities and changes from the earlier positions could be divined simply by scanning the books. The close connection to Freud persisted. One volume was titled *Freud and*

His Self-Analysis (Kanzer and Glenn, 1979) and a second
Freud and His Patients (Kanzer and Glenn, 1980). The first
addressed various features of Freud's many interests and
how they arose. The second contained contributions that
reviewed every one of Freud's long case histories, sometimes with a readiness to look at them somewhat differently—soft signs, perhaps, of movement away from
idealization of the leader. A third volume, *Lives, Events,
and Other Players* (Coltrera, 1981), featured psychobiogra-
phies. Many of these papers were inspired by the way
Freud applied his discoveries to historical figures, but were
further stimulated by some psychoanalytically derived
hypotheses about the lives of Luther and Gandhi, recently
published by Erik Erikson, who was then very much in
fashion. The last of the four volumes was more self-con-
sciously directed to treatment matters: *Clinical Analysis*
(Orgel and Fine, 1981). One section dealt with a variety of
disorders, many explained by references to psychosexual
sources, in which "orality" appeared prominently along
with "phallic–oedipal" determinants. A second section
dealt with developmental considerations. The expression
of the emergence of a vigorous child analytic training program, it included attempts to apply certain innovative
ideas, especially those derived from Anna Freud's thinking, to the treatment of children and adolescents. It is
unlikely that the word *subjectivity* appeared in any of the
papers of the volumes and certainly not in the sense in
which it is used today.

In contrast, the recent fiftieth anniversary morning
panel mentioned Freud only in passing or as an authorita-
tive buttress to an argument. Oedipality was raised once
by a panelist in order to dismiss its presence, and a second
time by a questioner from the floor who complained that
it might have been overlooked. Metapsychology was cited
briefly as a useful concept, but otherwise received little
attention. There was some attempt to introduce developmental perspectives but ambiguities dominated the concept, and there was uncertainty about its applications. By

way of contrast, object relations and subjectivity—important concepts these days—asserted themselves as major recurrent themes. This suggests that the direction the Institute has taken parallels, more or less, the course of changes in the psychoanalytic enterprise as a whole. This is almost certainly true, although the Institute regards itself and is still regarded by many others as a classical or traditional educational center. It would appear that subjects of contemporary scientific debate have considerable impact upon all psychoanalytic educational programs, whatever their roots. Perspectives inform clinical data; training informs perspectives; and zeitgeist informs training.

Introduction: The Volume's Concept and Its Development

Five psychoanalysts representing a spectrum of theoretical points of view and generations (all faculty members of the NYU Psychoanalytic Institute at New York University Medical Center) were invited to address the question: How do perspectives inform and misinform clinical data? Their replies contribute to an understanding of how contemporary analysts think—and why they think the way they do. Each analyst attempts to integrate the diverse, and potentially contradictory, models learned in training with the actualities of clinical practice.

Contrasts and convergences are best explored in the context of in-depth case material. For this reason Dr. Claudia Lament provided carefully detailed process notes of three consecutive sessions in the third year of a four times weekly analysis. She selected these hours because she regarded them as a turning point in a challenging treatment. By observing and reflecting upon her personal reactions she felt she came to better understand what had stood in the way of progress up to that point. Following her presentation, four other analysts, Mr. Nasir Ilahi and Drs. Kathleen Lyon, Peter B. Neubauer, and Shelley Orgel, discussed the clinical material.

The resulting exchanges illustrate the complexities of integrating the many influences in contemporary psychoanalytic practice. Four of the five participating analysts (Drs. Lament, Lyon, Neubauer, and Orgel) were trained, and continue to work, within a so-called traditional psychoanalytic model. Two of the panelists (Drs. Lament and Neubauer) had also been trained as child analysts. A fifth member of the panel, Mr. Nasir Ilahi, was educated within the British object relations tradition. All these training models share an appreciation of psychic conflict, differentiated structures, the effects of the past, and the intimate links between object relationships and development. At the same time there are differences, even within the so-called traditional group. Sometimes this is merely a matter of emphasis. However, there may also be more fundamental differences, for example, their views of therapeutic action.

The contributions of these five analysts convey how they think. We may note selective attention (e.g., alertness to nonverbal behavior, to metaphor, or other linguistic features) as well as preferred theories that affect their orientations. In addition to a contemporary Freudian perspective, there are influences arising from within the British object relations school, Anna Freud's concept of developmental lines, Mahler's (Mahler, Pine, and Bergman, 1975) separation–individuation theory, and Brenner's (1982, 1994) compromise formation theory (his elaboration of Freud's structural model). And by no means do these complete the list. These presentations also highlight the contemporary analyst's reflection upon his subjective experience, and the features that inform his "subjectivity" and "objectivity."

A number of questions arise: To what degree are different personal sensitivities and informing perspectives compatible or incompatible with one another? Do they only facilitate clinical work or can they also interfere?

In preparing this volume we considered the best format to explore these and other questions in the context of detailed process material. Too often panels are burdened by excessively ambiguous themes, unnecessarily personal confrontations, or time constraints that limit adequate discussion. Instead we imagined a panel that is well focused and permits ample time for its participants to elaborate and refine points of controversy and agreement. In addition, panelists successfully speak *to*, not *at* or *past*, one another. This volume is intended to simulate such a scientific meeting.

Chapter 1 consists of the panelists' original presentations in the celebratory panel described in the Preface. Clinical material is followed by four formal discussions preceded by our brief annotated comments. We also summarize spontaneous remarks by members of the audience and brief exchanges that ensued among panelists. For many readers there will be enough on this plate to be more than satisfying. The theme of the original panel is immediately apparent: multiple competing points of view, each perceived as valid. A secondary, although silent, theme surfaces: the potential hazards of asserting the validity of one's informing perspectives. The panelists, at least at first, are more inclined to use their time for explanations of their points of view. Rather than initiating a turf war, they prove comfortable with their different views, carefully measuring their comments but otherwise speaking in unrestrained voices.

However, as is typical of a panel lasting several hours, there is little time for a genuinely informative exchange of questions and ideas. To allow for greater depth and breadth we decided to "reconvene" the panel, not once, but twice. We provided the panelists with the texts of the original meeting, and asked them to further reflect on their own ideas, as well as the ideas of others. Their written responses comprise chapter 2. Some choose to further clarify misunderstandings, refine their earlier thoughts, and ask questions of fellow panelists, while others are emboldened to express positions clearly in opposition.

Their reactions were not only illuminating in themselves but raised additional questions that we believed to merit a second reconvening. In preparation for this we culled these questions, explicit or implicit, as well as our own reflections on them, noted apparent inconsistencies, and probed basic assumptions. This culminated in our circulating a letter to the panelists inviting each one to engage in one final attempt to refine, differentiate, reconsider or, if need be, join in argument to illuminate the principal topic and any latent themes that might seem appropriate. Their final contributions and our summary of the questions we asked them to address appear in chapter 3. (The letter appears in its entirety in the appendix at the end of this volume.)

Finally, in a brief Afterword, we consider some implications of the many questions and answers that fill the volume while posing further challenges. It should be noted that the usefulness of the book is a direct outcome of the effort and patience of the contributors who, at the end of the day, effectively spoke *to*, not *at*, one another.

Chapter 1

Clinical Material and Formal Discussions

EDITORS' COMMENTARY

In this chapter, a clinical presentation informed by one analyst's perspective is discussed by four additional analysts who offer sometimes complementary and sometimes contrasting points of view. The observations, formulations, and technical interventions proposed by the five contributors knowingly or unwittingly reflect their preferred theoretical perspectives.

Readers will soon note that the panel's primary focus, how perspectives inform clinical data, naturally encompasses a related question: How do perspectives misinform clinical data? It is no longer useful merely to determine which perspective is "correct." Psychoanalysis is an ever-evolving field. Early in its history Freud's understanding of psychoanalytic data was informed by the seduction theory. However, since he was "a relentless analyst . . . impatient with any given construction," as noted by another NYU Psychoanalytic Institute faculty member, Reisner (1999, p. 1029), Freud soon recognized the shortcomings of such an exclusive perspective and posed another: instincts and oedipal fantasies. Subsequently, these theories were also discovered to have shortcomings of their own in providing the necessary wide range of explanations.

A number of subtle issues arise in the careful reading of the panelists' statements. What are the opportunities and difficulties inherent in theory building? Why are orienting theories necessary? Are apparently conflicting theories partially or largely reconcilable; are they fundamentally as different as they initially appear to be? Are some theories more helpful at particular junctures of an analysis, or with particular patients? When is a theory reified, posing the danger that it altogether overwhelms data? Under such circumstances, sessions are transformed into mere confirmations of what an analyst already believes, and ex cathedra interventions are promoted that obscure, rather than illuminate, empirical observations.

Transcripts of the presentations follow, each one preceded by a brief introductory abstract.

THE CLINICAL PRESENTATION BY CLAUDIA LAMENT, PH.D.

Editors' Abstract

Dr. Lament's paper, meticulously articulate and carefully structured, represents her attempt to deal with a specific obstacle to progress. She initially abstracts historical data to be used as background to three carefully detailed consecutive analytic hours that illuminate the obstacle. Her presentation contains the observations she makes about her personal responses, a customary feature of contemporary writings. These observations include immediate responses, such as feeling devalued, memories of her own past life, associations to other patients, and constructions of her patient's early life that she freely acknowledges may not be accurate.

During this period of analytic work, Dr. Lament regards her patient's struggle with affective engagement as the principal obstacle that needs to be overcome. She has noticed that interpretations of dynamic meanings, comments about the threat of fusion, or inferred connections to the past have failed to promote that engagement. Shifting her attention, she comes to recognize that her examination of her own subjectivity moves her closer to the patient's feelings of despair and anger. This promotes engagement by enhancing her attunement to his experience, and thereby affirming its authenticity. Dr. Lament infers that these are pivotal hours, and implies that the serious obstacles to the treatment up to this point have been reduced by her activities.

Examination of her carefully elaborated process notes, including her observations of her patient and of her own personal reactions, provides an unusual educational opportunity for the student of analysis. What will the reader find engaging? And how will the panelists view Dr. Lament's procedures?

Dr. Claudia Lament

In this presentation, I will report on the details of three hours from an ongoing analysis. I will also include my thoughts, feelings, and reactions to what was going on in and between these hours, and what prompted me to intervene in the ways that I did. First, I will present an overview of my patient's background and the prominent issues that have emerged.

Mr. A is a 30-year-old writer and entrepreneur who was referred to me for analysis by a senior colleague who had treated him in once-weekly psychotherapy for six months. Despondent over the break-up of a love affair and beleaguered by a writer's block that had plagued him for several years, Mr. A sought help. Articulate and intelligent, he was serious and assiduous in setting about gaining a deeper understanding of his difficulties, and without reservation he agreed to a schedule of four sessions per week. I questioned how Mr. A felt about the ending of his psychotherapy; his responses were minimal. What emerged with most force was his intense preoccupation with the end of his love affair. Marion was a married woman with whom Mr. A had had a relationship for several years. He had begged her to divorce her husband and after many months of indecision, she stopped seeing Mr. A to save her marriage. Now, without her, he felt destitute and alone. Mr. A emphasized his feeling that their togetherness was a kind of melding together, a oneness and an uncommon sensual closeness that he had never before shared with anyone. "We were like twins in a way," he said, "we even looked alike."

The second problem, that of his writing block, was also a source of great misery. Despite his successful enterprise in a small business, Mr. A felt that his writing was the centerpiece of his life both emotionally and intellectually. However, he did not pursue his writing seriously; he avoided setting a regular working schedule to nurture his gifts, and distracted himself by tending to inconsequential matters which related to his company. In resisting an active pursuit of his writing, Mr. A felt that he was living but a shadow of an existence, with little value or meaning.

Several years before, he had been short-listed for a prestigious short story prize. The bare bones of the narrative concentrated on a thinly veiled account of his early adolescent experiences with a group of boys that emphasized their explorations in group masturbation. The narrative also chronicled his relationship with his best friend, a cruel and dominating boy whose stock in trade was playing off the insecurities of his companions, humiliating them, and finally threatening banishment from his clique. Mr. A was intimately bound to this boy and, when dropped by him, would attempt to recapture the boy's attention through a sullen, punishing withdrawal. In his associations, Mr. A spoke of his own masturbatory fantasies in which he imagined being penetrated by a woman with a penis or by an older man. During the analytic work it became clear that such fantasies (which he claimed were never realized in reality) and dream material that reflected his excitement in transvestites or older men occurred following some feeling of anger toward or disappointment by a woman.

The picture that I formed of Mr. A's family life was one of ever-present hostility, sometimes violently expressed, which alternated with a sense of emotional barrenness and futility. The second of three children, Mr. A described the family atmosphere as akin to a quarantined existence, where strangers were suspect and adventuresome forays into the world outside were perceived either as pretensions or as betrayals of the clan. The children themselves lived isolated existences apart from one another with little sense of familial warmth or feeling among them. Mr. A regarded mother as a female version of Dr. Jekyll and Mr. Hyde. Not without gestures of tenderness, she favored Mr. A above the other children, but what came through most forcibly in his reports was her relentlessly critical attitude toward him and her unpredictable fits and outbursts. He regarded her life as wasted; frightened and tentative with no knowledge of the world outside their isolation, mother's listlessness and sullen depressive states would dramatically turn into explosions.

As was customary, she took to her bed during the day and was often asleep in the afternoon when Mr. A and his siblings arrived home from school. Fearful of disturbing her, yet longing for contact, the boy would tiptoe to her bedroom door and quietly call out her name. Issuing from the darkness of the room were her screams, "Get out! What do you want from me! Get out!" Feeling that she never trusted him and always thought that he was up to no good, Mr. A described her insistent listening in to his phone calls which prompted him to install his own phone line. Yet, time and again, pressed by some inner need, he found himself sharing confidences with her only to discover to his dread—days or weeks later—that she would betray his secrets and use them against him. Heartbroken and furious, he retreated to his room and recited, mantralike, "Hate Mom forever," only to find himself a day or two later—longing to regain that special closeness—sharing his secrets with her once again.

Mother's relationship with father was also fraught and tumultuous; her fury toward him for his neglect of family obligations and withdrawal from domestic concerns was expressed in seething quarrels. Verbally abusive as well, Mr. A recalled how his mother would openly attack his father's masculinity, spewing out phrases like, "You take out your small penis every six months for my benefit?"

Mr. A's father was a highly regarded scientist who was, in his professional capacity, devoted to children who benefited from his research and beloved by the community at large. But in Mr. A's eyes such devotion to children was a sham, for there was not a trace of it in the As' home life. Although Mr. A was a superb athlete and prided himself on his many star turns, his father never appeared once to see his son score the winning goal. Choosing to work long hours, father was seldom home; when he was there, he buried himself in scientific journals. When he made the rare appearance, he was counted on to be fault finding and critical. But what Mr. A most painfully recalled was his father's complete and utter silence. He would sit expressionless in his chair as though not hearing a word of the boy's questions about the world, about life outside the walls of their home. Or, when the boy excitedly told of some new fact he had just learned, father would turn away or imply that Mr. A's learning was not up to par. In Mr. A's words, "Any bit of life in me, any shred of spontaneity, was crushed, quashed—my whole life! Life was not to be lived. There was a deadness in that house."

Gradually over the course of our work, Mr. A awoke to the realization that his own approach to life mirrored his parents'. "There's something wrong with how I meet the surface of my life. There's so much life out there; yet, I'm more comfortable clinging to being unhappy. What was bequeathed to me was miserableness. There is a pall over my life of not living." Sadly, he went on, "I remind myself so much of my parents. I'm not nourished and I don't nourish myself."

Over the course of the first year and a half of the analysis, as we worked on understanding some of the complex feelings which arose in the break-up of his affair with Marion, Mr. A fell in love with Rebecca. Although the relationship has been turbulent, Mr. A has felt deeply touched and moved. That Rebecca loves and cares for him feels miraculous to him, as he has begun to apprehend his feelings of being unlovable: "It moves me to tears when she tells me she loves me because it's as though I was never told it or that I don't believe it, anyway. But yet I want to hear it so much." Their sex life, however, is more troublesome, as Mr. A feels inhibited with her and resents that the sensual intimacy and feeling of oneness which he experienced with Marion is absent with Rebecca. He blames Rebecca for his lack of excitement, citing her inexperience with men as the cause, and finds himself withdrawing from lovemaking. He is loath to imagine that negative feelings toward her may be playing a part in his difficulty.

In the initial phase of our work, Mr. A was friendly and congenial toward me. However, once he felt some symptomatic relief his style of relating to me began to shift. I noticed he became freer in showing me other aspects, in particular hinting at feelings of hostility and devaluation.

By exploring my own reactions and Mr. A's behavior, I had the growing sense that he treated me as though I were a cardboard cut-out of a person, more of a thing that he could take or leave as he chose. Although it was true that he appeared to consider my interpretations at least on the surface, I felt that he used me more as a handkerchief to cry into which, when finished with, he would peremptorily discard. He consistently ignored breaks in treatment, and resumed our work as though we had never been apart. He told denigrating jokes about women, and became worried when he did not hear me laugh. Upon communicating to him my sense of his limited vision of me, he began to joke about a fantasy of seeing me as a prostitute. "Well, you are really, aren't you? I mean, I pay you. You? A real person? I didn't know that! I don't think about you—I mean, should I? Who are you to me? I pay you." His angry, sarcastic tone and laughter belied a deeper vulnerability and mistrust and I felt that we had touched on a most important, if not painful, core part of himself.

As our work continued, I became frustrated and increasingly puzzled by what was occurring. Mr. A would lay before me rich transference and dream material that seemed ripe for our mutual exploration. But as soon as I made what seemed to me to be a well-timed interpretation or remark, he treated my words as though they were penetrations, albeit ones that he invited. That is, he allowed me to "enter his mind" just enough so that he could, at will, triumphantly take control and expel me.

To add to this vexing situation was Mr. A's having been suddenly seized by an idea for a novel. Setting about it with a near frenzied intensity, it was to be a "literary reality show," in which Mr. A exposed his every thought and feeling over the course of a day, and then shaped these inner experiences into a novelistic form. He felt it would satisfy his desire to be seen in the most intimate detail—a kind of open analytic session with himself. As Mr. A put it, "This is the literature I want to write. I've put a lot of work into knowing myself and I can offer up that sacrifice in literature, a free revelation of identity. This will be what it is to be human." In his analytic hours, he spoke of its beautiful rawness: "all this sex and aggression is coming out. It's raw and crude—it's authentic and uncensored."

As if to entice me more, he made certain that I was not to hear a word of it. Dreaming of me as a deadly critic of his work, he kept me out of earshot of his novel. He turned instead to Rebecca as the confidante and keeper of its vivid rawness which, by the few hints he did offer up, sounded like the very stuff of analytic sessions he was not having with me. When Mr. A reported dreams of women who wielded knives aimed at his penis, I found myself interpreting his fears of me as a threatening, dangerous woman. But I soon came to the awareness that Mr. A mockingly discarded such interpretive efforts. And on at least one occasion he actually placed himself in the hands of a woman who, it appeared, was a prostitute. Following a session in which I interpreted his view of me as a dangerous woman who he worried might harm him, he involved himself with a woman in a bar who, beneath the tablecloth, unzipped his trousers and masturbated him. Afterwards in our session he excitedly told me of his exploits, as if to arouse me or to make me feel left out of his promiscuous liaison. But what rang more true was Mr. A's sense of emptiness, of hollowness that overpowered his words as he spoke.

Alternately, I found myself reacting to Mr. A's sexual behavior and talk in the hours by overinterpreting to him. In this way, I joined with the overstimulating atmosphere that Mr. A was trying to create, seemingly to protect himself from whatever he was experiencing on deeper levels.

But there was one occasion that seemed to provide a clue to this mysterious hollowness. An image from Mr. A's childhood arose and set me to thinking. As he struggled with his discomfort with his anger toward me, he noticed the way his hand clutched the back of the couch. Trying to peel his hand away, it snapped back to its place as though it had a life of its own, gripping the couch with even greater steadfastness. Upon observing his hand's iron-clad grip, he laughingly remarked, "It's like I'm clinging to a teddy bear."

The image of the teddy bear impressed me. My mind flashed to a memory of a little boy I once treated who was often furious with his mother. He clung to her skirts and tightly gripped her hand, as if holding on for dear life. What also appeared in my mind were images of how some little children freely pounce on their beloved teddies, even throwing, hitting, or smashing them; all the complex feelings of the loving and hating toddler seemed very much alive to me at this moment. And what child who is uncomfortable with his angry feelings toward his mother doesn't feel he must hold onto her for dear life? This image, I felt, was important not just to me but perhaps to Mr. A as well. However, I could not yet discern how the threads of my mind's wanderings knitted together to form a meaningful

pattern related to what was unfolding in our sessions. Co-
inciding with this was the complete collapse of Mr. A's
writing efforts. Sinking ever more deeply into his familiar
feelings of depression, he held fast to his conviction that
his life was meaningless.

It is in the throes of this work—nearly 2 $^3/_4$ years into
his analysis—that I will present three consecutive sessions
over the course of two weeks, a Thursday, Friday, and Tuesday. First, however, I will report on what happened in the
two prior sessions, as they provide an important backdrop
to what later emerges.

The first hour of the week, on Tuesday, Mr. A reported that he had had a difficult weekend. Rather embar-
rassed, he told of his strong reactions to having lost several
games of pool to a male friend: "It shouldn't have both-
ered me so much. But it did. I was furious at having lost
to him and I felt, though I may have been wrong, that he
was gloating over his victory." Mr. A then reported a
dream he had had that same night, in which this friend
owned a sleek, expensive sports car which Mr. A envied.
Having realized that his friend had paid a bargain price
for it, he tried to do the same but wound up striking a
deal that was less profitable than what his friend had ma-
neuvered. Although he possessed the car he so coveted,
he was surprised to see that his friend now owned something else that he envied as well and felt desperate to have.
The dream continued in this vein, with Mr. A adding,
incidentally, that the outline of his father had hovered
throughout. Frustrated and dismayed, Mr. A spoke about
his feelings of inadequacy with men until his thoughts wandered back to his father. He immediately returned to an
old resentment and hurt that his father never watched him
play sports, despite Mr. A's star achievements as an athlete.
In fact, the night before, while playing baseball in his amateur league, he caught a yearning within himself for someone to be there to watch him. As if to shake himself from
this feeling, he was gripped by a realization that he simply
must learn to play for the pleasure of playing for himself.
I noted aloud how quickly he moved away from his

yearning to be seen and appreciated, as if he had felt uncomfortable with those feelings. With that, Mr. A became
silent for several minutes. I broke the silence, wondering
what he was experiencing. He said nothing. I then asked
if what I said in our last exchange had prompted his clos-
ing off. He shrugged and returned to his silence until the
close of the hour.

In the following hour, on Wednesday, Mr. A smiled
coyly at me as he lay on the couch and lapsed into silence.
As the minutes ticked by, I shifted backwards and forwards
in my uncertainty. Should I break the silence? How long
should I allow this to continue? And, most importantly,
what had motivated this? I imagined that what was happening was connected to the hour the day before. But how,
exactly? My thoughts then drifted to Mr. A's coy manner
as the hour began. This sent up a balloon in my mind.
Might one reason for his resolute silence be his need to
make me feel small and helpless, while he seemed to be
triumphantly in control? Had he, in fact, felt small and
helpless in yesterday's session? Had my remarks engen-
dered this in him? Perhaps my intervention that underscored his yearning to be seen by his father as a star athlete
struck too painful a chord. Might he even have imagined
me as watching him?

Eventually I asked him if, in his silence, there was
something left over from yesterday that he was experiencing. He said nothing. I sat back in my chair and, as more
minutes ticked by, I felt increasingly puzzled and frustrated. Then, seemingly out of nowhere, I found myself
wondering if he wanted me to go after him. Before my
consciousness took hold, I found myself momentarily lost
in an imagining. What gradually crystallized before me
became an outline of a memory of myself as a child. In a
huff about feeling that I had been unjustly treated, I
stormed off to my bedroom where I sat all alone. But
I couldn't really want to be alone, I thought. And then I
realized that what I was doing was waiting, waiting for
someone to come to me and apologize, or at least to show
that they missed me. What I was really doing was waiting

to be found. Was this at all relevant to Mr. A or only to me, I wondered? Was he wishing for me to come and find him? Did he feel wrongly treated? I simply didn't know.

I then began to watch Mr. A as he lay on the couch. I noticed that he had constructed a kind of bridge by placing the fingertips of his two hands together. He kept them this way for some time. He then sighed deeply, collapsed them, and closed his hands together, placing them over his chest. As he did this several more times, the question occurred to me, was he linking us together and then taking us apart? I then noticed that upon unlocking his fingers for the last time, he closed and placed them over his genital area. This final gesture called up his oft-imagined picture of me as an attacker. Is this what he imagined I might be today, or was this how he had imagined me the day before? Was his silence now some echo of his father's cold, impenetrable silences? But why now? My consternation finally brought me to venture out on a limb. I wondered aloud that perhaps silence was the only way for him to communicate something important that he was feeling. Again, Mr. A said nothing and maintained this quietude for the remainder of the hour. As I watched him lie there, I felt a sense of unease, as if we were trapped with one another, locked together in silence.

The following are the three sessions which I will present in detail: Thursday, Friday, and the first session of the following week.

First Hour: Thursday.

Mr. A lay silent for several moments. Then, as if caught in a sudden tidal wave, I felt a rush of hurt, anger, and guilt pouring out from Mr. A's words. Last night, he said, he'd had a terrible fight with Rebecca. It was not his fault, he was quick to add. He was not to blame. Complaining of utter fatigue, he wanted to go to sleep early while Rebecca insisted on watching television in bed. "She was channel surfing," he said, "which made a strobe effect in the room. And those awful TV noises. She wouldn't stop so I just took the remote from her and turned it off." Then, in a tone of voice that nearly trembled for the great urgency that was boiling within him, he described that later that night, in her sleep, Rebecca attacked him with words of cruelty. "You know how she talks out loud in her sleep," he said.

> Well, I woke up and I heard her. She went for the jugular! It was a whole litany—I don't remember it all but she used the words *air conditioning* and *deductions*. The thing is, she hates air conditioning, and she knows that I do too, but I have no other space but my apartment to keep the products that I sell, and which have to be kept cool. And then, "deductions"—it's all to do with money and she hears me use that word a lot. Money informs our relationship in a big way. It doesn't destroy it, but it informs it and it's my vulnerable spot. She knows that and she was betraying me—using these things against me. She was mocking me! he said angrily. I felt so wounded.

He told of her attacks on his controlling manner, her feeling that their relationship is not characterized by a true sharing but rather by a lopsidedness; it's all on his terms, she lashed out. As if defending himself to himself or to me, he raged out loud, insisting this was not the case. After all, couldn't she recognize how tired he was? Couldn't she see his fatigue, his need for sleep? "There's no measure of her anger," he said, "Either it's full on or nothing. Going for the jugular like that—with money. It was such a betrayal. It's still inside me and I can't let go of it. Then telling me I was an old man because I wanted to go to bed early."

Feeling more sure-footed today that Mr. A's feelings were very much connected to me, I spoke. I said that he had been silent for the entire hour yesterday and for the latter part of our session the day before. Alongside what he feels toward Rebecca, might these feelings also have to do with something he's uncomfortable in experiencing toward me more directly? With an air of condescending dismissiveness, Mr. A replied that the connection I was making was simply tenuous. "Why would you say that!" he retorted. "What happened with Rebecca occurred after the session yesterday. Maybe it's true what you say, but it's reaching. Yesterday and for the last few days, I've been feeling very frustrated in my life. I do nothing with my life. I waste my life."

Despondently, he described his desire to make a film, his desire to be active, and to take charge of his life, but yet he feels a force within him that paralyzes. Speaking more softly now, as though to cushion a current of anger that was forming, he said, "I want encouragement from you. I don't expect it but that's what I want." With that, he fell silent. After a moment, he spoke again of Rebecca's intense anger, of its spewing out so. Unlike his own tendency to control angry feelings, her angry feelings are only waiting for an opportunity to get out!

I felt that the sequence that had just occurred—that is, his direct complaint that I offer no encouragement, his lapse into silence followed by his association to Rebecca's raging anger—all but cried out for an interpretation. But something inside me held back, as I had the sense that Mr. A, like his description of Rebecca, was just waiting for an opportunity to lash out. My intuition told me that were I to offer anything, he would spit it out. I continued to listen, as he suddenly remembered a dream that occurred after Rebecca's dream assault upon him.

He dreamed that Marion wanted him back and he wished to have sex with her, without having to reignite the whole relationship. He then recalled a second dream in which his car had flat tires. He realized that this dream must have been triggered by a recent, strange occurrence. While on a weekend jaunt with Rebecca, they had gotten a flat tire in an eerie, isolated, landscape, a blue collar area of a small town. "Then, some black woman appeared—as if out of nowhere. She freaked me out. She said she was from Triple A but I knew they'd not sent anyone. She had her hand in her coat as if she had a gun. I thought she might rob us. I was calm and cool, but really I was afraid. Then she asked if I was a cop and I said,

'Yeah, you better keep moving' and she left. We'd run over a dead animal—that's how my tire had gotten shredded.''

He then shifted back to his complaints about Rebecca and her selfish desire to go to the beach early the next day and neglect contending with his flat tire. "I'm riding on a spare!" he retorted. "I have to stop and get another one." He paused and added, "I'm angry that she can't see I feel used, she can't see that I'm really tired."

As we were reaching the close of the hour, I felt an intensity rise up in me to make him see that his feelings were profoundly connected to me. Although I heard a small voice warning me to consider more deeply what was going on, as I had been able to do earlier in the hour, I now succumbed to the urgency of my feelings. I found myself blurting out, "It seems it would make you uneasy to imagine me in these terms—as though I don't see your tiredness, how low you felt in our first hour this week. Perhaps you felt I didn't understand you. As though if you were to complain to me, I might lash out."

Predictably Mr. A spoke as if I had not uttered a word, yet his response was a direct hit to my blunder. Completely ignoring my interpretation, Mr. A spoke as though I had not spoken at all, and complained of how Rebecca had turned the tables on him. "Now she says that I'm not to watch TV if she's going to sleep. She's trying to start a war and I called her on it. 'You're doing that to be difficult,' I told her."

On that note the hour was over; as Mr. A walked out of my office, I felt chagrined and frustrated. Perhaps I should have left myself out of my interpretations, and simply stayed with his feelings about Rebecca or with his dreams, I thought. Or I might have underscored my being a potential betrayer of analytic confidences, much like the women he described today. In any event, I was the one being difficult; I was the one who wanted Mr. A to comply with my agenda due, in part, I suppose, to my own vulnerability about being left out and feeling forgotten. And, too, perhaps my own reactions dovetailed with a position Mr. A had been nudging me into by shrugging off my words.

That is, might he have been setting the stage for me to experience something that he had felt so often in his own life? My thoughts traveled further, as I then wondered if I were embroiling myself in a contest of wills with him in order to deflect my attention from somewhere else. And, if that were so, where was that somewhere else that I did not wish to see?

Second Hour: Friday

After some minutes of silence, I offered, "It doesn't feel comfortable to say what you're experiencing?" "I guess," he replied, tiredly, "I don't know why I should speak. I don't feel close to you. Maybe I think you don't care. It gets tiring to speak. Yesterday you didn't give me any perspective or anything." I remarked that he sounded disappointed in what I had to offer. "Maybe," he replied. A sense of despair began to creep into his words as he told of his doubts as to whether he could resolve anything in his analysis. Feeling no progress, it seemed an impossibility to be separated from his problems.

In this vein, Mr. A spoke of Rebecca's wish to buy an apartment with him. As a note of helplessness registered in his voice, he reflected, "How much she wants a structure in our relationship, and how incapable I feel in doing that, of being that open and committed in a relationship. I don't know how to do it. I have such big walls up around me." Just last night, he and Rebecca had another huge fight, where Rebecca refused to let him speak.

> That's what upsets me so much. She won't hear my side, she won't hear my words. And she told her mother about our fight. Of course, her mother thinks she's right and I'm wrong. Eventually, as we fought, we both cried and cried and it was hugely cathartic. I said how I was so upset because she won't let me speak. We were so angry we nearly broke up. I felt she just wanted to punish me and not let me have a say. She believes I don't understand what she sacrifices for our relationship, that so much of our

relationship turns on what I want. When I could let myself see her feelings, then I could address what the whole thing was about and we came together again. But for how long?

After a pause, he continued, "These walls in me. I don't know how they're supposed to come down. In here or anywhere." I then offered, "You had hope that I could help you yesterday. Perhaps you had an idea as to how I could bring those walls down?" Angrily, he snapped, "I don't have any idea about what you could give me. I equate you with this process. My life is ridiculous. I do nothing with meaning." Despising the uptown life in its isolation, he spoke of the paradox of his incapacity to move downtown, where the atmosphere is warmer, where there are cafes and restaurants to wander to and feel welcomed by. As my office is also downtown, it now struck me that Mr. A was expressing his desire for something solid and real from me, not merely analytic nourishment. Perhaps that is what he imagines will make the walls come down, I thought. As he went on, I felt his earlier note of hopelessness now resonating more deeply, filling the room with heaviness. "I wonder if my existence is plagued by restlessness and self-consciousness," he said. "Language seems futile to me. As I try to describe an aspect of my experience, it comes at the expense of every other truth. To speak, to use speech, seems fraudulent." With this, he fell silent.

In these moments, I felt an urgency to call out to him. How much I wished to make an impact with my words and arouse in him some curiosity about his state of mind! But this was just the problem, I thought to myself. I saw that at this moment, words were utterly meaningless to him. Feeling a glimmer of understanding that something of great importance was below the surface, I no longer felt myself in the throes of a need to deliver him, but could endure my witnessing of his experience. Listening again, I felt the pain of a deadened existence, the blast of his desire to end the analysis and to give up: "I don't know why I'm here or if I should keep coming," he said. "I see

no happiness around the corner, anywhere. You could
bury yourself in meaningful work and not worry whether
you're happy or not. I don't see my relationship as making
me happy, a family making me happy—nothing. I don't
want to abandon the relationship, but what is the purpose
of all this?''

With a backward glance as he left—that to me spoke
volumes of his contempt for my uselessness—I felt sharply
my own sense of helplessness. Sinking into my chair, I felt
a wave of futility sweep over me. Then, emerging almost
seamlessly from this state of mind, I saw a little boy lonely
for his mother tiptoe up a flight of stairs through a long
hallway toward a darkened bedroom where he knew he
could find her. It was then that I saw a dead, sleeping
mother lying there, unarousable, untouchable, surrounded by impenetrable walls that would not come down.
Tentative, peering out into the darkness, I saw the child
call out to her, all the while knowing the answer that would
await him: "Get out!" Here too, lying silently, I saw the
dead child, lifeless, like her, yet fused with her, alive with
her. And when the silence was too much, the closeness
more than enough to bear, there were always the words
of provocation, of accusation, of secret betrayals or the
"realness" of sexual excitement to end the closeness and
the deadness. There then appeared a third presence, a
form which became a ghostly outline of a man who buried
himself in meaningful work for the sake of other children,
whose eyes never saw his son score the winning goal, whose
not-there-ness and belittling silence steeped the air
around me.

Rousing from this reverie, I saw that in this hour, the
shadows cast by these figures had shifted from him to me
and from me to him. The realness that Mr. A seemed to
be wanting from me, perhaps the only way that trust could
be imagined with another, now resonated profoundly.
How difficult to feel the yearning for someone you need
so deeply, yet the very person whom you feel you cannot
trust! Now, too, the weekend had come, and I realized

that these images and feelings that I was experiencing mingled with my earlier visions of a furious boy clinging to his mother's skirts, of a child's rages visited upon a beloved teddy. Perhaps for Mr. A, keeping me close in these complex ways was the only ending possible, the surest way of being found, if that were to happen at all.

Third Hour: Tuesday

It was the first session of the new week. He is ten minutes late. Again, Mr. A was silent and made another bridge with his fingertips, broke it and sighed deeply. He then said, "You should just start the session by asking, 'So, what's going on?' " I asked, "Why should I do that?" "To get the ball rolling," Mr. A responded, and then, with added sarcasm, "I guess then there's the pretense of being interested?" I felt strongly his anger and his hurt, and I was thrown back to my reverie after the Friday hour and to the separation of the weekend. He went on: "I had a tough few days. I felt hopeless and I got screwed in business by somebody yesterday. On the weekend I had terrible dreams, a succession of them. In one of them I was being hunted by Nazis. I felt frustrated and so ambivalent toward Rebecca. She didn't seem attractive to me and I felt so distant. There's no way I can sustain a relationship. No way I can have kids. It seems important for other people. Not for me. I'm so riddled with problems. There's no climbing out of it." He then spoke of how he had shopped in an overpriced supermarket that carried low quality foods. Rebecca wanted to bake a chocolate cake, but he dissuaded her, saying, " 'How can you? With this quality?' I can drop a fortune in a good restaurant without it bothering me but I can't spend a cent in a cheap supermarket without it killing me."

He went on, in a way that seemed like a spewing out at me of random unhappiness and despondency. He spoke first of having gone out to dinner with Rebecca. He didn't feel like spending money as he felt so undeserving. "Business is slow and I don't do meaningful work. But when

Rebecca said she'd pay for the dinner I lightened up. I guess she read me a little bit. But I hate feeling this way." He continued speaking, if carefully: "I also had the realization last night that you can't help me. In a way I'm angry. Not at you, but frustrated. No one can help me. No one. No one can make this go away."

He then remembered a dream in which his writing tutor had found a tape of him having sex with Rebecca. What upset him wasn't to do with his teacher's having been witness to his sexual performance, it was that his teacher had betrayed him and stolen a tape from his bedroom. Reflecting no further on the dream, he dropped it and darted quickly to his report of how an old business colleague had betrayed him.

> He's such a little boy. Anyway, he's not paid me for a long time although I've sent him invoices. I knew he'd pay me eventually, but I didn't like his tone of voice, the way he was saying he wouldn't pay me unless I issued him a more recent bill. I objected to the way he spoke to me and left him several very angry messages. He then withdrew all his orders from me because he felt I betrayed him. I called him and said, "C'mon! Don't you ever have arguments? You don't just end things like this! Cut it out!" But he made up his mind that he'd screw me and he did.

Heaving a heavy sigh, Mr. A fell silent. After a moment, I said to him that it was as if he experiences me as not recognizing him in his aloneness, in his deep despair; he feels that really I don't care. How can he trust my words? After all, over the weekend I had really left him alone to contend with these feelings. Perhaps, now, for the second time in his life, I am another woman who has betrayed him, who is sleeping, who is surrounded by great walls that will not come down.

After a moment he said, "There was that silence there, before you spoke just now, and I felt your silence greatly. Until you spoke. I felt I just spewed out all this randomness—like a catharsis on my part—but I got no insight. And I felt foolish after. And angry. Like nothing was really achieved by my speaking. It was not a catharsis, really. Like I spoke for the sake of not being silent. Like I threw out all this noise so that you could put some of this together for me." Pausing for a moment, he spoke again, "As Rebecca lives with me, I see myself more clearly. It's upsetting to see yourself. You can't hide. It's depressing when you realize what you're like. I wonder if everyone is riddled with all this." I said, "As though you feel so alone with what's inside you." After a moment, he associated, "Rebecca has so much inside her that she doesn't see. She seems to become another person at night—a terrorized person who comes out in sleep. Every night. Then I think about people who have kids and get married. It feels natural for them but so impossible for me. I feel it's too much what I'm going through." With a heaviness that barely allowed the words to come through, he said, "It seems existential in some way. It's not something that can be discussed or remedied." I offered, "It feels beyond words." He lay quietly and the session was over.

I think that what was beyond words for Mr. A was the terror of his childhood. His remedy of this terror was also something that he felt could not be dispensed in language. Yet, in these final moments, I think that Mr. A was able to render words with meaning. That is, he was able to own some part of what he had been feeling during the hour—his anger and resentment and desire that I pick up the pieces of his world—but had simply heaved out at me. Then upon his recognition of these feelings, he appeared able to share with me, in a genuine way, his despair and hopelessness. It felt to me that in so doing, the walls had come down, if only a little. I venture to say that Mr. A had taken a small, yet important step toward beginning to trust the presence of someone who does not provide tangible offerings, but who can tender the realness of understanding.

What I hope to show is not simply Mr. A's difficulty in reaching those places within himself that haunt his life. It is my difficulty, too, in reaching into the past of Mr. A's lonely, rageful and frightening childhood. It is a past that was, in one sense, all too well known to me—but one that I had, in another way, resisted knowing at all. In and between these hours, allowing myself to experience it anew, in a different register than I had before, enabled me to grasp what before had been ineffable. Although my imaginings about Mr. A's early childhood experiences were my constructions and not his, they acted as a stimulus to me to contact him in a way that I believe is more authentic and more true to his experience.

DISCUSSION 1: KATHLEEN LYON, M.D.

Editors' Abstract

Dr. Lyon is attracted to a concordance between the panel's topic and Dr. Lament's difficulty with the patient. The panel attempts to explore how perspectives inform clinical data. Dr. Lyon demonstrates that, at times, perspectives more than inform data; they create data. She calls attention to a secondary theme in the panel. The same patient may comply with the preferred orientations of different clinicians, she notes, and appear dissimilar as a result. Thus Dr. Lyon believes that perspectives are useful but that they may also interfere with therapeutic work. She urges awareness of orientations as an important therapeutic tool, and suggests a need for flexibility. Perspective, she says, should be a work in progress, not a fixed position.

Turning to the case, Dr. Lyon examines what she regards as a central dynamic: the patient's dilemma about being too close or too far within relationships. Each position threatens both the patient himself and the interactive partner. In suggesting that in this case the analyst's capacity to revise her perspective permitted the treatment to move forward, Dr. Lyon provides a compelling case for recognizing that perspective not only informs clinical data but may also misinform observations.

Dr. Kathleen Lyon

Dr. Lament has offered this panel an unusually open and detailed case report. She generously describes not only her perspective in working with this patient, but her private reveries and feelings as well. In doing so she provides rich food for thought with which to consider the panel's topic, "How Perspectives Inform Clinical Practice." I was particularly intrigued by the panel's title because, although at any moment in my own work I obviously have a particular perspective that I bring to bear on my listening, I also feel that my perspective is very much still a work in progress.

I had an experience as a resident that has some relevance to this morning's panel. The hospital at which I trained had a history of long-term inpatient treatment for schizophrenic and borderline patients, but was at the time in the middle of an institutional power struggle. This centered around the perspective of a new attending who diagnosed many patients, previously seen as borderline, as having multiple personality disorder. A patient admitted to my unit was an intense, angry, depressed woman, struggling with suicidal wishes and self-destructive actions. I was able to arrange that she have diagnostic interviews with both a well-known analyst who treated severely character disordered patients, and the MPD maven. Perhaps not surprisingly, two wildly different phenomenological pictures emerged. I was fascinated by this demonstration. To say this woman's suggestibility and compliance were important determinants of her experience is a gross understatement. My concern was that the style of both the interviewers seemed to exploit, rather than respect, this. They attributed the differences in the patient's presentation to errors in the other's perspective, rather than to a dynamic between their convictions and the patient's vulnerabilities.

I have since then particularly appreciated the opportunity that analytic work provides to be sensitive to and curious about the effect an analyst's perspective, style, and technique have on the way the patient presents. I do not think that we co-construct the patient's reality, or that the interaction between analyst and patient is even the primary focus or locus of change. But I do think our perspectives influence what we see and how we work, and that this in turn can influence the way our patients meet us psychologically in their efforts to understand their minds.

In the clinical material presented, Dr. Lament generously provides us with sensitive and compelling data regarding many aspects of the work, including her struggle to understand and reach a patient in great difficulty and pain. She is impressively attuned to her own attitudes and perspectives, and allows us to witness how she felt she and the patient affected each other, and how her responsiveness to this allowed them greater understanding and access to each other. Unlike the interviewers from my residency, Dr. Lament allowed her experience with her patient to change her perspective and approach, dramatically, and in a way that I think will be crucial to the patient's progress in his analysis.

In the clinical material, the analyst describes work with a patient in a second phase of his analysis. The early, seemingly productive working together has been replaced by a difficult, angry, and entrenched transference neurosis. The analyst elaborates her puzzlement as the patient becomes more and more unreachable, first with a coy and subtly devaluing stance, then by viciously rejecting her.

As I read about Mr. A my attention centered on several things. I wondered about this patient's need to see the analyst as nothing, his clinging to despair, and, of course, how his destructiveness toward the analyst relates to his past relationships with his mother and father. How could the interaction of approach and withdrawal between the patient and analyst, described in the clinical sequence, shed light on this?

I was also intrigued by Mr. A's attempts at writing and his use of this activity in the analysis. He is suffering from writer's block, conflict about writing. I wondered how his first story, described as a "thinly veiled" account of his adolescent experiences with group masturbation and his friendship with the sadistic friend, play into this conflict. Perhaps he wrote this story in an attempt to deny his guilt and anxiety about these experiences, and these affects being known. Afterwards, he is frightened about what he revealed, which prevents him from writing more. Mr. A's next attempt, which takes place while in analysis, involves a similarly exhibitionistic display, in which the conflict over being seen and revealing his sexual and aggressive thoughts is played out in the act of not telling his analyst the details. In fact, I think this man, who despairs of words being of any use between people, cannot fully use his writing as a way to communicate with another. He uses his writing in part as an exhibitionistic act, the equivalent of a sexualized physical exposure, and falls victim to the associated conflicts.

In addition, Mr. A is struggling with intense anxiety over separation and individuation, amply demonstrated in the sadomasochism in his relationships, of which the adolescent friendship is an important example. I think this friendship and his experience with group masturbation exemplify aspects of the clinical material we have heard. Although it is not stated that the sadistic friend was included in the group, it is safe to assume that some of the fantasies and dynamics that fueled the group masturbation were active in the relationship with the sadistic friend. This experience was important enough to the patient that he wrote about it.

Where is it in the analysis? We know that Mr. A fantasizes being penetrated by a woman with a penis or by an older man, and that dreams expressing excitement in transvestites or older men follow anger or disappointment over experiences with women. The analyst tells us that she began to feel that he experienced her interpretations as penetrations that he could triumphantly expel. At this time he also embarks on the novel, which is obviously exhibitionistic in its form and content. It involves no other objects, just himself and his inner thoughts, in all their sexual aggressive crudeness. In this description the novel

has a masturbatory quality, in that it is a compromise between isolation and connectedness. The feelings that are
experienced are his alone, experienced alone, but there
is a fantasized other who is involved in some way.

Who is the analyst in the scenario? Perhaps in part
the analyst is in the role of the mother. Mr. A both desperately wants to separate from her, and yet also wants closeness; he is terrified of destroying her in either case. To
attempt to remedy this dilemma, he does several things.
He expels her, as she expelled him, simultaneously keeping her through identification with her and rejecting her.
He puts the analyst in the role of a third-party listener,
listening to his talk about his novel, as his mother listened
to his telephone conversations. He wants mother's closeness, but he cannot experience his sexual longings toward
her. He invites her in to witness and, likely in unconscious
fantasy, to participate. Consciously such participation is
anathema.

Perhaps this provides clues as to why Mr. A must consistently reject the analyst's participation in his analysis. If
her participation is experienced unconsciously as a form
of sexual involvement with him, he must reject it to avoid
terrible anxiety and guilt. It is clear that his dreams of
women wielding knives at his penis would lead the analyst
to feel she is a threat to him—as indeed she is. Perhaps
he is also placing her in that role in his dream as a punishment for his wish to be sexual with the mother-analyst.
Thus he assumes a less threatening, more passive, role.
The analyst further tells us that during this time she peri-
odically finds herself overinterpreting to him. In this sense
she feels she is joining in with the overstimulating atmosphere. She suggests that this may be in the service of Mr.
A' s need to not look into deeper feelings. But it may also
be the other half of what I'm suggesting: the participation
the patient is conflictedly inviting, conflicted precisely because of its sexual and aggressive meanings to him.

Mr. A's relationship with his adolescent friend provides other clues to his behavior in sessions. We know that

when he felt cast out by this friend, he responded by withdrawing and hoping to attract his friend's attention, again by his absence. I believe this may be, in part, what the analyst is responding to in his withdrawal from her in the clinical vignette. I would like to take up the sequence of sessions provided, and add my own thoughts as I do so.

In the first session, Mr. A describes events and dreams that relate directly to his fears of inadequacy as a man. He loses at pool, and dreams a friend has a better car for a better price than Mr. A can maneuver. He associates to his feelings of inadequacy and to his father. He then speaks of his yearning to be seen and admired when playing baseball, but feels he realizes that he must play for his own pleasure. The analyst intervenes, commenting on Mr. A's move away from the feelings of yearning for admiration, wondering if he is uncomfortable with those feelings. The patient is silent for the rest of the session. Although I have no doubt that the analyst is correct in thinking that Mr. A is uncomfortable with his longings for admiration from father, clearly he is not able to use this defense interpretation at this time.

Why is that? The silence continues into the next session, as the analyst's mind wanders over the possible reasons for it. She finally feels a connection with the idea that he wants her to go after him, and associates to her own childhood attempt at connections through withdrawal. She wonders if he feels attacked by her and studies his body language. She wonders if he links and delinks them in putting his fingers together and taking them apart.

Again, I think what is at work here is the adolescent experience. I do think Mr. A wants her to go after him, but that now he experiences her as the sadistic friend, with whom issues of separation and individuation are closely bound—the adolescent elaboration of the same issues with mother. In this frame of mind, I believe he experiences her defense interpretation as both an attack and a threatening seduction, undermining his attempts to see himself as a strong independent man. He is trying to present himself as self-sufficient. The analyst's interpretation, focused on his discomfort with needing father's admiration, in effect draws his attention back to his more infantile wishes. He may hear her comment as a taunt, effectively saying that his discomfort is a sign of weakness. Perhaps I would have commented on the patient's dilemma, his difficulty in wanting both to be admired by others and to be independent from them.

In the next session Ms. A's anger at his girl friend seems to confirm how enraged he feels at the analyst, and attacked by her, even betrayed. He and his girl friend are locked in a power struggle symbolized, no less, by the television remote control. His view of her sounds like a version of his experience of his mother. "There's no measure of her anger. Either it's full on or nothing" (p. 13). He is hurt and frightened, and feels tired and in need of understanding and care. He sounds more like a little boy. When the analyst wonders if these feelings have anything to do with her, he cannot allow that it is so; he berates her and himself.

Mr. A regresses somewhat under the force of his feelings. As his next comments show, he now seeks closeness again with the mother-analyst, despite his overt rejection of her. He tells the analyst that he wishes she would encourage him.

This is followed by Mr. A's dream of having sex with Marion without having to "reignite the whole relationship" (p. 14). I read this as a wish for the blissful fusion he imagines he experiences with her. Instead he gets a real relationship, symbolized by the next dream: getting a flat tire. In a real relationship he is threatened by feelings of inadequacy and fears the potentially dangerous woman, the threatening woman with the gun. In the analyst's next comment, she wonders if Mr. A imagines that she does not see his fatigue. Perhaps he feels misunderstood by her; maybe he is uneasy experiencing her as more understanding than he does. But he will have nothing of it and he refers again to the "war" between him and Rebecca. In her reflections after this hour, the analyst wonders whether she has enacted a need to push her agenda. This is a thought to which I would like to return.

In Friday's session Mr. A is despairing and feels alone. He fears he can't be in a relationship. He and Rebecca have had a big fight. She wouldn't "hear [his] words" (p. 16). Only when he could let himself see her feelings was there any repair. When the analyst again tries to wonder if the patient wished she could help him bring down his inner walls, he reduces her and himself to nothing: "I don't have any idea what you could give me. I equate you with this process. My life is ridiculous, I do nothing with meaning" (p. 17). Here I think he describes the only, albeit costly, way he could remain with mother: to be empty, nothing, despairing, as she was. He goes on to despair that language is meaningless, and he has no hope of analysis ever helping him.

At this point the analyst moves out of her previous need to "deliver" Mr. A from these feelings. She feels she can be with him, "witnessing" the truth he feels in his words. Here the analyst has made a crucially important shift of perspective. She is able to feel with him more than before. If I had been able to recognize this at the time, I might have reflected to Mr. A that he and I were both nothing, together. Or in a similar way I might try to emphasize the attempt to be with me, while simultaneously destroying me. As the patient leaves, the analyst has another reverie: that of the little boy looking for his depressed, deadened mother, down a lonely darkened hall, only to be thrown back by her angry words. She sees the deadened child fused with the deadened mother. She imagines the outline of a distant, cold father over it all.

In the last session reported, Mr. A begins by spewing out anger about betrayal. This time the analyst simply reflects that he feels betrayed by her and left alone. How can he possibly trust her words? There is no comment about anxiety, or defense against it, in her intervention. He can hear and accept this and talk about how upset he is to see his own shortcomings. He continues to describe how impossible it is for him to be in relationships, and then associates to Rebecca becoming a terrorized (and to him, terrorizing) person at night. Heavily, he says his isolation is existential, not something that can be discussed or remedied. "Beyond words" (p. 21), the analyst interprets.

Several interesting possibilities emerge in these last few sessions. I think after feeling thwarted in, or unable to maintain, the defensive posture toward the analyst that recreated his relationships as an adolescent, Mr. A regressed and began to experience a more fully developed maternal transference. There are several important factors here for him.

Certainly, Mr. A felt mother to be unmanageable and untrustworthy in her depressive rages. He now feels relationships to be impossible because people are untrustworthy, unbearable, and unpredictable in their anger. I think his conviction that relationships are impossible for him is also rooted in an identification with his mother, for whom this seemed to be true as well.

This prompts the question, what is it like to be the child of a mother for whom you are unbearable? All children are vulnerable to the concern that their anger or needs are too much for their parents. Mr. A regularly experienced this as a fact. When his mother was depressed, any child would have been too much for her, and he was no different. Is it a reasonable speculation to think he felt toxic to her at these times? Relationships would then be impossible for him from both sides, as he must have had to maintain his distance to preserve the object and himself. The only other alternative for a young child is to be with mother, not as a separate individual but as an extension of her. Psychologically fused with her, he would provide no threat to her.

What happens to words between two people who are fused psychologically? They are used in the service of maintaining the fusion. In a parent–child relationship, the parent is the object that creates and transmits meaning. We have all likely witnessed the painful spectacle of a controlling, poorly individuated parent dominating a child through the recasting of the child's words into shapes and meanings that suit the parent's needs. "No, you didn't mean that" is a not uncommon but deadly rejoinder. The child suffers a form of gaslighting; his faith in his feelings and the capacity to find meaning in words is damaged. The patient says, "To speak, to use speech, seems fraudulent" (p. 17). Words are a means of asserting one's own mind, and without sanction to have one's own mind words are destroyed.

The analyst wonders at one point if she is the one trying to be difficult, the one trying to push her agenda. This is an extremely important perspective in working with Mr. A. He feels all his relationships are based on meeting the terms of the other and, in extreme situations, being fused with the other. The only way to be a separate individual is to be in isolation from others. The analyst is trying to connect. When the analyst interprets the patient's perceptions of her as based on anxiety and defense, he does not hear this as simply an observation. He hears an implication—one which enrages him—that in order to be in a relationship with her he must see her differently, according to her own need. Mr. A hears her asking him to see her differently than he does. When the analyst stops trying to "deliver" him, she no longer feels the need to break down his walls. He no longer feels required to trust her, and he relaxes. Her interpretation at this point is subtly but importantly different. Rather than including an observation about affect and defense, it is closer to an empathic acknowledgment of his state of mind. She has heard his words and has not tried to make them different.

I do not mean to imply that such empathic contact is sufficient for the analysis of this patient. At some point Mr. A will need to put this transference into words and analyze it in order to tolerate a true relationship between two individuals. To do this, however, will require tolerating enormously painful feelings and memories. This is another reason why the analyst's subtly shifting attitude in the sessions is so important. She reaches a state of mind by the end of the sessions in which she feels able to tolerate and witness his great pain and despair, simply to be with and to contain his feelings. This is essential if Mr. A is ever to believe that he can bear his feelings while trying to move beyond them. He needs to have the hope that his experience can be borne and to feel confident that he need not shield his analyst from anything, as he had to shield his mother.

For Mr. A, rather than offering interpretations regarding his anxiety about the analyst's dangerousness, or his fear of needing her, I would instead emphasize the impossible dilemma he experiences in trying to be with her at all. For him, any closeness is experienced as overwhelming, and any distance as destructive, to both parties. The best solution he can come up with is to struggle for power in relationships. The analyst is able to shift from defense interpretations which he experiences as controlling criticisms, to a more empathic stance in which she can feel and contain his dilemma rather than try to demonstrate her understanding of him. Then Mr. A can feel less involved in a struggle with her, and more able to focus on his own state of mind.

I wonder if he perceives this shift, not only through the analyst's words, but also as a result of nonverbal communication that he must rely on as a substitute for words. I have no doubt that the inner work that the analyst did in between sessions gave her a sense of greater confidence and contact with her patient. Mr. A would have been searching for signs that he was not harming her. I think the life of her mind must have been communicated in the life of her bearing, and he knew she was safe. At the same time as her interpretative stance and her psychological bearing toward him shifts as a result of what he says to her, he is able to perceive that his words did have an effect on her, that they did communicate something important of him to her. Mr. A's prior experience would lead him to feel that only with great intensity and rage can he get through to another, if at all. But this leaves him again terrified that he is too much for another to bear.

Mr. A must do his best to tear his analyst down, and to feel certain that he cannot succeed in doing so. One way to do this is to tear down meaning, to reduce words to nothing. In this way, feeling that words are useless may be partly motivated by his need to be destructive. In order to make use of his analytic experience, he must analyze his terror of separation from mother, his fear that leaving her or staying with her will harm her, and his identification with her rage and despair. To be different from mother is the ultimate way of leaving her. He must create his own path in relationships, and learn to trust his own feelings and needs. Compliance and opposition are no longer enough. Mr. A must create his own meanings. For this he needs words. For this he needs analysis.

DISCUSSION 2: SHELLEY ORGEL, M.D.

Editors' Abstract

Dr. Orgel also stresses separateness and connectedness, although from the standpoint of the unrecognized effects of interventions and silences. He proposes that the specific hours Dr. Lament offers represent a turning point for the treatment because the influence of speech and silence are increasingly accessed. Both the analyst and the analysand move toward an effective working relationship. This patient sees separateness as abandonment and connectedness as fusion. Such threats cloud the value of communicative speech or of silently attentive listening.

Carefully reviewing the sessions, Dr. Orgel observes how Mr. A progresses toward tolerating the aloneness that comes with the acknowledgment of others. He argues that the therapeutic action guiding such movement—at this stage of the analysis—springs primarily from the form of the experienced exchanges. This is mediated through speaking and silence, rather than exclusively through the substantive content of the interpretations or reconstructions offered. Dr. Orgel's discussion focuses on the theory and technique of the management of patients such as Mr. A so that they may be delivered to the other possibilities of psychoanalysis, where words are used to discover meanings. A close reading of this discussion should enhance the therapeutic tools of any clinician.

Dr. Shelley Orgel

It is a pleasure to have read and to discuss this sequence of analytic sessions. They represent, I believe, a crucial turning in the winding road of this analysis. In these days, Mr. A moves tentatively beyond his hopelessness and despair, risking becoming a patient in analysis. Simultaneously, Dr. Lament also faces her hopelessness and despair, choosing to immerse herself unguardedly in deeper waters of emotional understanding of herself and her patient as she proceeds in her rocky, scary process of becoming more fully what she can be as an analyst. This report tells us about the separate and interlocking progress two individuals achieve—for themselves and each other—as one becomes more fully a patient and the other more profoundly an analyst.

I shall try to show that these sessions represent a mutually experienced turning point. The patient becomes able to tolerate the connectedness in separateness that enables him to speak to an analyst who is perceived as more than projections of parts of self, or as simplified versions of early part objects. Concurrently, and by no means coincidentally, the analyst has become more able to tolerate the disorienting separateness that accompanies listening without prematurely offering "help" and comfort to her patient. She abstains from using spoken words to demonstrate that she is whole and present, that she has sympathetic understanding of his plight and possesses an analyst's capacity to interpret. She has been able to absorb the patient's teaching that both speaking and silent listening may express *and* create distance and closeness, absence and penetration, hate and love.

Mr. A indicates the central importance of speaking versus silence, and merging with objects versus separateness and absence, in his statement of the two issues that brought him to treatment. One is loss of Marion with whom he had felt melded as his female "twin," and without whom he felt destitute and alone. The second is his writer's block, his "silence" of several years, the loss of his creative voice, leaving his life now "with little value or meaning." His short story and his associated fantasies also focus on such alternatives. He achieves completion through union, or endures desolate aloneness in sullen withdrawal. Mr. A's fictional persona achieves wholeness through an intimate bond with a boy, by participating in boys' group masturbation, or by being penetrated by a phallic object. (Does Marion's husband represent her phallus to Mr. A?) Such actions protect him from being cut off from the group, from the pain of being rejected by his best friend in adolescence, or in later years by a woman. We might speculate that his fantasy life is pervaded by the wish to become invincible and invulnerable to rejection and desertion, by either a man or a woman, through imagining ways of becoming both male and female in one. "[Being] locked together in silence" (p. 12) with his analyst includes such meanings, I think. As the analysis stirs up his object hunger for another, the delicate stability that this fantasy allows is endangered.

Hearing Dr. Lament's report, we quickly become aware of the centrality of conflicts in Mr. A's past life over speaking and silence, as gratifying or threatening in his core relationships. For example, in the afternoons his mother protected herself from the noise of contact with her children by remaining silent in her bedroom as they returned from school. The boy's quiet calling of her name, a tentative waking touch of a hungry child, brings screams: "Get out! What do you want from me? Get out!" (p. 5). He will shake his analyst with his reenacted version of these encounters. As mother, he will silently scream at her, during what Dr. Lament calls at one point his "resolute silence" when she dares to approach him, especially with mollifying, comforting interpretations of, for example, his yearning to be seen and appreciated. Or another example: Mr. A indicates that being listened to, especially by an unseen person, can feel intrusive too. His mother's listening to his private conversations led him to install his own phone line. He created a wall of silence against her attempts to hear his secrets. But the wish to talk to her, probably to her above all, about these secrets repeatedly overrules his judgment and brings about numerous betrayals by her.

Furthermore, what Mr. A "recalled most painfully about his father was his complete and utter silence" (p. 6). Father's sitting expressionless in his chair as though not hearing a word of the boy's questions, not responding at all to attempts to engage him through words, will also be repeated in the analytic situation. Mr. A becomes the aggressor through his silent withdrawals, provoking in the analyst frustration and futile urges to overinterpret.

I want to note that he experiences as *annihilations* both his mother's attempts to silence him and his father's greeting his approaches with absent silences: "My whole life [was crushed]" (p. 6), he says. "Life was not to be lived" (p. 6). His experience of a negation of his being within this "dead" house and his awakening into existence in a new place—in a new kind of relationship—describes one version of the movement occurring in the clinical sequence of the three sessions.

In the earlier unfolding of the transference, as Dr. Lament realized, partly through exploring her countertransference reactions, Mr. A perceived her as lacking depth—without dimensionality—as if she lacked an "inside" in which he might seek and discover valued and longed-for structures and capacities. He could not bear knowing that she was indeed a person, a woman, a whole object he longed to keep, someone he could miss whenever he had to confront inevitable evidences of her separate existence. In these earlier days and months it appears he could not appreciate her except as a transitional object—part self, serving part functions for him—as a handkerchief to cry on, as a teddy bear to clutch onto.

Although Mr. A's central idea for his novel appears to be a displaced representation of his analytic sessions, these are shaped into expressions of himself excitedly exhibiting before a silent, admiring, sexually turned on, undifferentiated audience. This is a mirror image rather than an object—an image that would be fragmented if he had to cope with a person whose response he did not command or dictate. He attempted to gain the reassurance he sought in the transference in his interlude with the anonymous woman at a bar who masturbated him under the table. In this period of analysis, Dr. Lament reports she reacted by overinterpreting to him, "joining in the overstimulating atmosphere that Mr. A was trying to create" (p. 9). I wonder if she did not also need to affirm through her interpretations her *presence* and identity, for both their sakes, in the face of his vengeful attacks on her very being. One can see these attacks—*his* version of "*Get out!*"—*both as projections of his own emptiness and deadness, and an identification with his mother's rage-filled denigration and expulsion of the boy he was, and the man he would become (her image of father).*

Now I'd like to discuss a few aspects in the sequence of sessions which led into what I believe was a qualitative shift in the course of this analysis.

The Tuesday Hour

It begins with Mr. A's envy of more powerful males and the forlorn hope that he can be watched by a silent, admiring other (in Kohut's term *a self-object*). It is only in her reflections in the following hour that Dr. Lament wonders: "Might he even have imagined *me* as watching him?" (p. 11). We can't know what would have followed if she had included herself in her interpretation of his discomfort with his yearning to be seen and appreciated. However, by imposing silence on her, he achieved a version of his wish for a mirroring object. He *did* get her to watch him, and to sit by quietly as he played by himself. Similarly, he forced her into frustrated silence in the way he introduced his novel written, I believe, *for* her, but about which he will not speak *to* her.

As I read this part of the report, it brought me back to a wonderful paper I had recently read, Poland's (2000) "Witnessing and Otherness." As you think over Dr. Lament's report and this and other discussions of the material, perhaps Poland's ideas will resonate with them as they did for me. He writes of:

> [The action of the analyst as a witness, one who recognizes and grasps the emotional import of the patient's self-exploration in the immediacy of the moment, yet who stays in attendance without intruding supposed wisdom—at least not verbally. . . . This silence of engaged non-intrusiveness rather than of abstinence, this listening in a way other than to seek for what can be interpreted, complements the analyst's interpretative function [Poland, 2002, p. 18].

The patient's asking for witnessing reflects, Poland adds, "[his] advancing self–other differentiation, both a growing self-definition and an increasing regard for otherness, seemingly separate processes that are intrinsically unitary" (p. 18).

Poland asserts convincingly that witnessing and interpreting exist in a circular relationship. I believe that Dr. Lament's patient helped her to realize increasingly clearly what I regard as a profound truth about the psychoanalytic process and relationship. In Poland's words, "No matter its helpful or even kindly quality, an interpretation implies a powerful statement of negation and separation deeply structured within it, a negation central to the analytic process" (p. 27). And he concludes: "The negation buried in an interpretation exposes and strengthens essential otherness" (p. 27).

Now to the Thursday Hour

This follows the "silent session of Wednesday" in which the analyst felt as if she and Mr. A "were trapped with one

another, locked together in silence," unable to break free
of each other—yet. A great deal is going on in this hour,
but I'd like to isolate and follow the meanings and uses of
speaking and silence in this and the next sessions. When
Mr. A in this first session speaks about Rebecca, we are
alerted to consider his communication as a guide to the
transference. And what happened with Rebecca? She
wouldn't stop "those awful TV noises" (p. 12) so he took
the remote from her and turned it (her?) off. Rebecca
attacked him with *words* of cruelty. He says that her *talking
out loud* in her sleep was going for "the jugular. . . . I felt
so wounded" (p. 13). Rebecca attacked his controlling
manner and said their relationship, which was all on *his*
terms, lacked true sharing. Mr. A's needing to go to bed
early, his intense need for sleep (represented by his withdrawal into silence before the end of the session?) made
him an old man (impotent like father as depicted in mother's harangues). Rebecca clamors to wake him; she *refuses*
to be silent. Her actions tell us what his analyst—if she
weren't an analyst—might have been provoked to enact
with him the day before (including, perhaps, complaining
that he was not paying her enough?). Most visibly, we see
Mr. A warding off the raging mother by identification with
the aggressor. In fact, he is both the sleeping mother and
the unreachable father who protect themselves by direct-
ing their annihilating, silent absence at the analyst, as the
child who dares to speak.

The transference interpretation Dr. Lament makes
concerning his discomfort is accurate, I believe. But Mr.
A's retort, "Why would you say that?" (p. 14) sounds to
me as if he feels awakened abruptly by someone who shatters an unconscious fantasy of merger by objectifying herself, who becomes distant and unreachable because she
speaks. Her interpretation comes before he has included
her representation in his inner world with sufficient
strength and stability for him to be able to hear her voice,
to tolerate her speaking to him from outside. And at this
moment in time and in his analysis he is close to being
unable to bear, in Poland's words, "the negation buried

in any interpretation" that "exposes and strengthens (his) essential otherness" (Poland, 2000, p. 27).

The Friday Session.

These themes were continued the next day. He says, Rebecca *does* want him. But he puts up walls against her, we think, as a representation of the active, *speaking* analyst, because he feels she won't let *him* speak. She won't listen to him. She won't hear *his* words, he says. He feels Rebecca, in speaking, takes away *his* voice, negates him, while she feels he takes away *hers*. (Rebecca is also equated with the silenced analyst.)

When Dr. Lament speaks of wanting to help Mr. A in his isolation, she is letting him know indirectly that she is a separate person with her own feelings. His response is to negate her angrily. He says, in effect, I do nothing with meaning. You, merely a figure representing this process, are therefore nothing. He moves toward the nihilistic idea that speech is fraudulent. Truth (the possibility of oneness with the other) is destroyed by speaking. Truth, defined by him as identity, union between the self and object, is only possible in silence. And so Mr. A falls silent.

Dr. Lament's report captures the inner life of her patient as a child as it is reemerging in the analysis. And she movingly conveys her complementary need, a core part of *her* identity, to communicate *understanding* with her words, to use words to awaken him to an object world that neither shuts him out (shuts him up) nor violates or wounds his self-representation. As she increasingly appreciates through *her* emotions what it means for him to offer and receive words, she acquires a patience to hold back, to endure witnessing his experience without having to satisfy her own self-defining need to "deliver" him. One could say that her becoming patient enables Mr. A to be a patient.

Her word *deliver* here is so pregnant with meaning. Not to have to deliver him means she accepts his needing to remain inside her, in a wordless space, until he becomes

ready to move outside, into a realm where incomplete connectedness, the aloneness of otherness, prevails, and absence is imperfectly and unreliably bridged only by
insubstantial words. She becomes able to allow Mr. A to
remain, as mother had not, in her darkened room without
shouting "Get Out!" For him at this juncture, her benign,
careful, caring words must have sounded like bombard-
ments of "Get Out!" Or, as Dr. Lament adds, they became
transformed into "words of provocation, of accusation, of
secret betrayals or the 'realness' of sexual excitement to
end the closeness and the deadness" (p. 18).

Finally, the Tuesday Hour

It begins in a different way. This day Mr. A will help her
by telling her how to speak. He talks at length, I believe
feelingly, of his unhappiness, his inability to sustain sexual
and loving feelings for Rebecca. "There's no way I can
sustain a relationship," he continues, "no way I can have
kids" (p. 19). (Perhaps he expresses his nascent awareness
of his identification with the mother who casts her children out of her room.) Mr. A's refusal to spend money in
an overpriced supermarket with low-quality food evokes
an image of the oral rage and clamped-shut mouth of the
infant whose mother's tempting breasts failed to give
good, nourishing milk. This is also a reference, I think, to
his refusal to take in and give out in the analytic relationship.

Then comes a pivotal moment of the session and possibly of the analysis. Mr. A says carefully, "I also had the
realization last night that you can't help me. In a way I'm
angry. Not at you, but frustrated. No one can help me. No
one. No one can make this go away" (p. 20). This is an
apparent reference to a primal scene experience and
dream, and a betrayal by his writing tutor follows. Then
he tells about a business colleague's withdrawal from him
because he sent the man some angry messages about pay-
ments due him. He called the man and said, "C'mon.
Don't you ever have arguments? You don't just end things

like this. Cut it out!" Mr. A goes on: "But he made up his mind that he'd screw me, and he did" (p. 20). Mr. A then falls silent.

As I reached this point in the report, my immediate response was that these sessions were announcing a new beginning of this analysis. In the course of this *"No"-filled* session, especially in the five negatives I've just quoted, a new self was crystallizing. We hear Mr. A's despair yield to sadness, his alienation beginning to give way to loneliness, and the rage that destroys the object becoming modified by ambivalence. Tolerating feeling painfully separate from Rebecca has enabled him to see himself more clearly, he says. He now is looking at Rebecca, and I believe the analyst, as another, a very different person from himself, and from the parents of his childhood—not a mirror image—and so he is freshly able to look into himself.

That Mr. A can talk meaningfully to the analyst about his conversation with his disgruntled business colleague indicates he is beginning to believe that a sustained, ambivalent relationship may be possible for him. The repeated "no ones" in this session announce, if such a thing exists in analysis, a moment of breakthrough, a smashing of walls, his expression of negation that marks "the beginning of a self apart" (Poland, 2000, p. 27). The "no one" who can help Mr. A must be someone who will submerge her identity to his when necessary; a relationship to ideas of empathy and partial temporary identification is implied. Such an analyst feels no angry impatience to deliver (externalize, objectify) him through her activity, her interpretations. She will allow him to emerge in his own way, in his own time, into the mournfulness of a real analytic relationship. As she does, he becomes open to and able to tolerate interpretations that show him that even from her position of otherness she can "get" what he means; she can know him, if only approximately. And so he may be able to move toward accepting, even seeking the possibility that their shared language may create a bridge of love from and toward him as a separate, unique being.

In this third session, when Mr. A falls silent, "heaving a heavy sigh" (p. 20), Dr. Lament feels he is inviting her to speak. The heavy silence, his and hers, now seems oppressive to him. Dr. Lament emphasizes that he feels he cannot trust her caring words because she really did leave him over the weekend, betrayed him, and is herself sleeping surrounded by walls that will not come down. In doing so she is recognizing in words their essential linked humanity, even as she asserts that they both must recognize and accept their separateness. If they do, they may attempt to reach each other through words now rendered meaningful, if always inadequate. As Mr. A says, "It seems existential in some way" (p. 21). And the analyst then says with words as perfectly attuned as words can be, "It feels beyond words" (p. 21).

There will of course be many days ahead when words will be just noise, for catharsis alone, fillers in the silent, empty space between them or instinctualized substitutes for bodily penetrations and interpenetrations. And silence between them, with its many meanings, will sometimes seem urgently necessary. But I believe that as a consequence of this rich analytic sequence, their relationship will have changed irrevocably for both analyst and analysand.

DISCUSSION 3: M. NASIR ILAHI, L.L.M.

Editors' Abstract

Underscoring the essence of the primary theme, Mr. Ilahi believes his perspective to be informed by the impact of object relations on growth in general, and pathological outcomes in particular. He believes that he and Dr. Lament (as well as the other panelists) look at data from considerably different theoretical models, and consequently see different underlying narratives. Mr. Ilahi's views are very much influenced by the work of Melanie

Klein, while he believes Dr. Lament is more oriented toward ego psychology. A careful reading of Mr. Ilahi's discussion provides a useful primer for anyone who has found difficulty grasping the Kleinian theory of object relations.

From the vantage point of his perspective of archaic infantile anxieties inspired by actual parental behavior (e.g., their dark anal–sadistic side), Mr. Ilahi constructs a narrative about unrecognized infantile helplessness. He adds that such helplessness is not accessible to the patient, precisely because it has been experienced at a time when words are not available. While Dr. Lament uses her subjective experiences to find a way to promote affective engagement, Mr. Ilahi suggests that such awareness can be put to better and more specific uses. By recognizing that an analyst's feelings represent projections of the patient's childhood experiences, along with those of his parents of that period, he can decode narratives and offer them as interpretations. These provide the optimal basis for therapeutic action.

In his discussion Mr. Ilahi imparts a vivid description of an important theoretical perspective. His approach to the clinical material, as well as the contrasts he presents between his own and Dr. Lament's views, illustrate the principal theme of the panel and its subtler subtext.

Mr. Nasir Ilahi

I feel both privileged and delighted to be participating in this exciting panel. Dr. Lament has provided us with a very interesting and moving clinical account written with great personal candor, and I would like to thank her very much for so generously and courageously agreeing to share this material with us.

It is well known that a number of different theoretical systems have come to exist within psychoanalysis over the last several decades. As Sandler (1976, 1993) has pointed out, certainly so far as the international scene is concerned, until perhaps the 1970s or early 1980s "each school tended [to see] their own theories as the 'right' ones and to see those . . . [of others] . . . as being, to say the least, misguided" (1976, p. 1097). Since that time, however, there has gradually been a growing process of dialogue and mutual interaction between the proponents of different theoretical points of view. I see our panel today as contributing toward this very worthwhile effort. I agree with Sandler (1976) when he says that to quite an extent analysts today have increased their "capacity to view [their] . . . own and other people's theories as theories which can be modified rather than fixed systems of belief" (1976, p. 1097).

However, while there is much to celebrate in this respect, my experience of such dialogues—especially between viewpoints that at a deeper level diverge widely from each other—has also alerted me to how incompatible understandings of clinical material, and technique and interpretations that arise from them, can sometimes be. This is not the place to go into any detail about the many factors, including historical and cultural ones, that give rise to such significant variations. While discussion at forums like the one today are helpful, perhaps the best arena to become clearer about divergent approaches is in an ongoing clinical seminar where proponents of different viewpoints can discuss in detail their responses to clinical material.

With these preliminary remarks, I will proceed to my discussion of Dr. Lament's presentation. I recognize that my perspective is very different from the one implicit in her report, and also from those of the other panelists this morning. My comments may, therefore, sound perplexing. However, they are offered in the spirit of exploring the more divergent side of theoretical pluralism that I referred to earlier, with a view to promoting mutual interaction and debate.

In my discussion of Dr. Lament's material, we should also bear in mind that it is she, as the analyst, who is in the arena with the patient. Therefore, she has direct access to the full impact of being there, far more than can ever be put into a clinical report. Any understandings that I may be able to offer are necessarily from a considerable remove, and therefore have inherent limitations.

Before discussing the detailed sessional material I would like to make some observations about Ms. Lament's background account of the analysis which she has very ably summarized for us. First, the analyst describes how Mr. A blamed Rebecca for his sexual difficulties, including his considerable sexual inhibitions, in contrast to the blissful feelings of oneness that he experienced with his previous, married lover, Marion. He attributes Rebecca's inability to excite him to her lack of experience with men. Now this communication can be understood at many levels; it seemed to me that here he was probably expressing what he felt in the transference. We know that he had seen a senior colleague for psychotherapy for six months before being referred to Dr. Lament for analysis. I assume that Mr. A is aware that he is seeing somebody less experienced than his previous therapist. (Incidentally, I wondered, for reasons that become clearer later, whether this previous person was a female or male, and also whether the reason for the referral was that Dr. Lament could offer a lower fee for analysis than the senior colleague.) Thus Mr. A could be talking about his lack of emotional stimulation in the analysis. This he sexualizes, as he tends to do with almost everything, as a concrete defense against feelings. Blaming this on the analyst's lack of experience, he idealizes the previous analyst. Many negative feelings about the analysis are simmering below the surface, even though Mr. A remains outwardly friendly and congenial toward the analyst.

Dr. Lament describes how, after the initial phase of the treatment, she began to feel used by Mr. A as a thing—one he can denigrate and discard as he wishes. She became increasingly frustrated and puzzled by what was occurring. This situation became even more difficult for her as he began to mention his new novel. It seems to me that the analyst felt both teased and tantalized by references to all sorts of uncensored material that was going into the novel. Worse still, Mr. A was discussing the very stuff of the session in detail with girl friend Rebecca but not with the analyst.

Here I would disagree, as I believe the very stuff of the analysis was taking place right in the transference-countertransference, and was not to be found in the factual details of the novel. Let me explain. It seems to me that Mr. A was unconsciously evacuating the child part of himself that was tantalized, and then painfully denigrated and excluded by his parents. He has very powerfully described how he learned not to trust his mother, who partially responded to him but then suddenly undermined and expelled him from her mind—and literally her room when he would return from school—and a father he experienced as both withdrawn and castrating. Mr. A now feels very excluded by the analyst, presumably over his inability to have emotional access to her. He deals with this internal state of affairs by denial and splitting off of this very needy child part. He projects it onto the analyst in such a way that the *analyst* experiences a mixture of being shut out, tantalized, and frustrated, while Mr. A identifies with the rejecting parent. All this takes place unconsciously, and is vividly lived out in the transference. However, it is at a level that is *beyond words and beyond his individual associations*. This is a type of transference communication that an analyst can only decipher through the careful monitoring and working through of the affects being aroused in him or her by the patient, evaluating these in the context of the rest of the patient's material.

If my understanding is correct, then the analyst's task is to find ways that will facilitate the patient's recognition of what is taking place. This involves grasping how his early history and problems are being lived out, and reflecting on the very painful states that are being desperately evacuated, as they are unthinkable. As previously stated, *this* would be the very stuff of analysis at this stage.

What I am referring to is a way of understanding transference and countertransference phenomena which, to my mind, provides access to the more archaic and infantile parts of the patient that are beyond words. This derives from an object relations framework for understanding such phenomena that is *significantly different* from the more classical American ego psychological approach apparently being employed by Dr. Lament. As I hope will become a little clearer further on, the two approaches can lead to the unfolding of analytic scenes and dialogues that diverge considerably from each other.

From my perspective, Mr. A's analysis is replete with unthinkable anxieties, fantasies, and conflicts. These may outwardly look more neurotic, but underneath desperate and intense defensive measures are at work to ward off these anxieties. This way of functioning contributes to transferences, such as the one just outlined, that appear very bizarre and confusing in their own right unless they can be deciphered.

Tuesday Session

In this first hour of the week Mr. A began by reporting his difficult weekend in which he had felt very bad about losing several games of pool to a male friend who gloated over his victory. He then narrated an interesting dream from the same night in which he envied this same friend's sleek, expensive sports car. Having realized that his friend had paid a bargain price for it, he tried to do the same, but wound up striking a deal that was less profitable. Although he now possessed the coveted car, his envy did not end, as the friend now had some other desirable possession. This process continued, leaving him, it seems, dismayed and frustrated.

Mr. A mentioned that the figure of his father hovered throughout. His associations were about his frustrations with his father who never watched him play sports or witnessed his star achievements. The night before he had felt a strong yearning for someone to be there to watch him while he played baseball in his amateur league.

At this point, I had a strong impression that Mr. A's immediate real concern was his experience of the analysis—vividly portrayed in his dream—that was clearly disturbing to him. My thoughts here are derived from my practice of scanning the patient's verbal and nonverbal associations for allusions that may have a hidden link with the situation between us. Everything that the patient says is first evaluated on the assumption that it also refers to his feelings about me—in other words to determine what may be taking place in the transference in that particular session. In general, I am especially interested in how what the patient is talking about or enacting may link with what has transpired in the previous session. The continuity between sessions at an unconscious level was especially emphasized by Melanie Klein (Klauber, 1981). More specifically, in the very first session after a weekend break or a vacation (or the sessions before such a break) I am particularly interested in assessing in my mind the patient's way of dealing with this important experience in his internal world.

It seems that Mr. A experienced the weekend break as a type of a humiliating defeat, in which he has to be on his own, while his analyst (now representing his father) is not there to watch him or be interested in him. Further he feels it is the *analyst* who gloats over this triumph. He envies the things that his analyst-father has which, however hard he tries, he cannot really possess. As the dream shows, this leads to increasing frustration and dismay. At one level the sleek, expensive sports car represents an envied perfect–omniscient penis that the father-analyst is believed to possess. This is something Mr. A feels he does not have (he loses in "pool" repeatedly and only plays in the "amateur" league), but which could, if he owned it, magically protect him from all the feelings of narcissistic vulnerability, inadequacy, and humiliation that he experiences at such breaks. It would also seem to stand for his expectations from the analysis that he is getting at a bargain price (both in terms of the possible low fee, as well as the low emotional price that he feels he pays as he holds back his vulnerable, dependent feelings). Mr. A would like to use the analysis concretely as an omniscient penis that will protect him from feelings of smallness, impotence, vulnerability and, to the extent that he is developmentally an adult, presumably also homosexual anxiety. This does not work, however, as these feelings are still there. Further, Mr. A seems to feel that the *analyst* has some way of keeping *herself* narcissistically protected (with her analytic sports car–penis) that he feels insulates her from any such feelings; he is frustrated that his own search for this is constantly elusive, no matter what he does.

To escape from the painful feeling of wishing that someone were there to take an interest in him, Mr. A tells himself that he must learn to play for his own pleasure. In other words, he desperately tries to strengthen his narcissistic shell. When he becomes silent for several minutes, Dr. Lament asks him what he is experiencing. However, it seems to me that at this stage it is beyond Mr. A's capacity to consciously and directly express what he is feeling via his individual associations. Much of this had already been communicated, quite clearly as I see it, in an unconscious manner. It is now the *analyst's* task to decode this communication and to take the dialogue further. If Mr. A could have consciously verbalized all this, as Dr. Lament's question implies, then he would be a far less disturbed patient functioning at a significantly higher level of development, with much less need for analysis. As it happens, Mr. A lapses into a silence. I have the impression that the rest of the session, in which nothing is said, is very difficult for both patient and analyst.

As I discussed in relation to the themes emerging in Mr. A's analysis prior to these sessions, Mr. A deals with his profound feelings of inadequacy by projecting the needy and impotent parts of himself into the analyst. He thereby attempts to gain an illusory sense of control and adequacy. We can see from the material of this session how despairing he feels when this defensive maneuver breaks down over the weekend. There is a powerful need in him to regain his psychic balance by putting a wall around himself; in this session he concretely excludes the analyst through his silence.

Wednesday

Mr. A begins this session with a silence. Dr. Lament notes astutely, I believe, that he smiled coyly as he came in. She does not know what all this is about. But then she begins to wonder if this is connected with the previous session, whether he felt small and helpless at that time. Again her opening intervention in which she asks Mr. A about whether his silence is connected to something being carried over from the previous session does not achieve anything because it does not address what is being enacted in the session. Dr. Lament describes her feeling of frustration that, as I have suggested before, is primarily the frustrated and helpless part of Mr. A of which he is trying to rid himself. He does so unconsciously, by getting her to feel as he does so that he can triumph and feel coy.

Dr. Lament's next thought is related to her childhood memory of storming out and waiting for someone to pursue and apologize to her, reassuring her that she is missed. She wonders if this is what Mr. A is going through. Following what I have said earlier, in my view the content of Dr. Lament's memory of her own experience is of a very different order. It is from a higher level of organization compared to what is taking place inside Mr. A; given the nature of his disturbance, he is using desperate measures of an archaic nature to shore up a sense of himself. This, I believe, has not been recognized by the analyst and can therefore give rise to very difficult and confusing counter-transference feelings. Nevertheless, the fact that her mind wanders away from him at this very difficult moment of a silent session could be an important projective identification. It may be indicative of how *Mr. A* deals with painful states in his own mind, which becomes clearer, as I see it, in the next session.

Dr. Lament's puzzlement about what is transpiring continues in what must be a very difficult experience for both patient and analyst to bear, as Mr. A remains silent for the rest of the session.

Thursday

Some very interesting material appears in this session. After a period of silence, Mr. A erupts into talking about his "terrible fight" with girl friend Rebecca. He is anxious to add quickly that he is not to blame for it. He describes a scene in bed with her just after he conveyed his desire to sleep early, as he was very tired. As she channel surfed, a disturbance was created by awful TV noises. When Rebecca would not stop, Mr. A grabbed the remote from her and turned it off. I wondered here whether he felt underneath that Rebecca was dissatisfied with him sexually and emotionally. To his mind, she has now dealt with this by satisfying herself with her own narcissistic devices (channel surfing), sadistically cutting herself off from his needs. This infuriates Mr. A, who attacks by snatching the controls and depriving her of her imagined narcissistic gratifications.

Later he mentions that Rebecca attacked him with words of cruelty in her sleep, going for the jugular. He could only remember the words *air conditioning* and *deductions*. From these words he comes to the conclusion that she is attacking him in her sleep. She hates air conditioning. While he also hates it, he needs to cool his apartment because of his business products. *Deductions* is a word he uses a lot; he feels money informs their relationship in a big way and destroys it.

It seems to me to be fairly clear, if one is to follow the line of thinking I have indicated thus far, that Mr. A is talking not only about Rebecca but also about what is taking place in the transference. I believe he felt that the analyst was, in her silent thoughts, very dissatisfied with him, and that she felt attacked by his withholdingness when he was in bed (couch) in the previously silent session. He experiences his withholding primarily in sexual terms, as he sexualizes everything. But it clearly has many other deeper levels relating to his feelings of emotional coldness and impotence. Mr. A then feels that the analyst retaliates by forgetting about his needs, occupying herself with her own thoughts in those silent periods when he is trying to isolate himself from her. In other words, he believes the *analyst* goes "channel surfing" in her own mind, and abandons him this way.

I think this is a projection of how Mr. A deals with situations when he feels excluded (creating his novels with masturbatory themes, the "literary reality show"). I find it very interesting to consider, as I discussed earlier, whether Dr. Lament did to some extent actualize this in her countertransference ruminations the previous day when Mr. A silently excluded her from his mind for most of the session. At this time her thoughts wandered away from him to think about memories from *her* childhood.

Mr. A then feels unconsciously that the analyst will also viciously retaliate against him—"go for the jugular"—and accuse him (in her silent thoughts, if not explicitly) of being emotionally cold ("air conditioned") and financially withholding ("deductions"). As I have indicated before, financial withholding in his mind is linked with emotional withholding, which is his way of both defending himself and attacking. This sets up talion fears from his internal objects, now projected onto the analyst. It also contributes to his feelings of guilt, that are of a persecutory nature, rather than the more mature type of guilt that one would associate with the depressive position (Klein).

Incidentally, Mr. A's remark that he, too, does not like air conditioning, but is compelled to use it for business reasons, is an important unconscious communication. The healthy part of him is not happy with the coldness of putting walls around him but is forced to do so by other parts of him. It is *this* healthy part that is unconsciously seeking help from analysis, as it is caught up in severe inner conflict with other parts that undermine and paralyze him.

At this point the analyst is also able to perceive that Mr. A's feelings in relation to Rebecca are very much connected with the analyst. She asks Mr. A if this is so. In my view, like some earlier interventions during the week, this question seeks *individual associations* and can only be aimed at the more adult part of the patient. It also remains at a very general level. Mr. A is unable to see any specific links with the transference that could provide conviction, and so he dismisses it. He proceeds to express despair that his life is being wasted.

Although his thoughts now turn to making a film and to moving on in life, he remains paralyzed. As he continues to feel absolutely terrible for his internal attacks on the analyst and her feared retaliation, which have not been addressed in the session, he must seek external reassurance from the analyst that he frames as "encouragement." Nevertheless he remains internally terrified of retaliation from the analyst, and characteristically displaces it onto Rebecca.

Two interesting dreams are then related. In the first dream, his previous lover Marion wants him back; he wishes to have sex with her without having to "reignite" the whole relationship. In the second, his car gets flat tires. His associations to the second dream lead to a black woman who terrified him, as he thought she might shoot him with a concealed gun over the weekend when his car had an actual flat tire. He thought his tire had shredded as he ran over a dead animal. He then complained about Rebecca who is preoccupied with her own concerns about going to the beach, oblivious to Mr. A's flat tire problem as well as his tiredness.

The analyst does not tell us her thoughts about these uninterpreted dreams. However, it seems to me that in the first dream Mr. A is struggling with the issue of how to have some form of intercourse with the exciting part of the analyst (Marion) that he sexualizes, without having to engage any feelings. He is terrified that, were he to do so, things would explode inside him and her (i.e., get ignited). This theme is followed up in the second dream, as he feels impotent-deflated (flat tires) when he is unable to have a proper relationship with his object. I believe the fear of being attacked by a woman with a weapon over the weekend is related to the phallic mother aspect of the analyst who is terrifying and persecutory, especially over the weekend break. Confronted with this separation from the analyst, Mr. A is especially prone to attack and murder her in his mind (the dead animal) because he feels neglected and uncared-for by a self-absorbed maternal object. However, this attacked object then eerily returns in a persecutory form as a murdering phallic mother (the black woman). We know from Mr. A's history that he felt a lot of violence and explosiveness in the family expressed by his mother who terrified and castrated his father in numerous ways including sexual belittling.

The analyst does interpret the bit about whether Mr. A's feelings about Rebecca's lack of concern and understanding are linked up with his feelings about the analyst. However, to my mind this touches the surface of his concerns; it does not address his intense anxieties that I believe he has clearly been attempting to convey unconsciously in a number of ways in this and earlier sessions. Nevertheless it is interesting that Mr. A totally ignores what the analyst has to say. In this way he seems to be enacting a psychological murder of her in the session, a theme that is latent in his dreams and associations. As the session ends, the analyst is left feeling angry, frustrated, and to some extent self-blaming. One can consider that the analyst's feelings here are also those that have been deposited with her unconsciously by Mr. A in his attempt to escape from these very feelings himself.

I do not have the time to comment on the detailed reports of the Friday and the following Tuesday sessions. It seems to me that the same themes that I have drawn attention to above reappear and remain, along with heightened despair and hopelessness—a feeling that his life is slipping away. I will, however, make some brief observations about the Friday session.

Friday

In this session Mr. A says that despite the isolation of uptown life, he paradoxically does not have the capacity to

move downtown where there are welcoming cafes and restaurants. Dr. Lament correctly infers he is talking about
seeking something from her, in her downtown office.
However, contrary to what she then states, I do not believe
that he is necessarily asking for concrete gratification as
opposed to analysis. It seems to me that he is wondering,
at a deeper level, why he continues to stay in that part of
his mind where he has built walls around himself. He iso-
lates himself (the uptown life) instead of moving to the
warmth and healthy nourishment that is available to him
outside, in the good feeding part of mother and in the
good feeding part of the analyst (the move downtown).
What he does not understand—and the place where analysis can help him—is the arousal of intense primitive anxieties within him from the dark (anal sadistic) side of both
his parents and himself. (I have alluded to these in some
detail earlier.) This will emerge should he emotionally
come out of his well-defended state. It is his unconscious
fear of these places which keeps him trapped (emotionally
uptown, as it were). His sanctuary protected by walls has
become a prison, a theme that often appears. If he cannot
work through this—and the only place where there is any
possibility of this ever happening is in the transference—then he feels everything is pointless, and there is
no end to his despair.

In conclusion, I have tried to illustrate rather briefly
some of the differences in the psychoanalytic narrative
that I hear in contrast to what Dr. Lament describes. These
different narratives originate from the *considerably different*
theoretical models to which she and I subscribe, implicitly
or explicitly, in our respective clinical endeavors. These
reflect our divergent backgrounds and training. Differences in clinical understandings can also arise, even if analysts share the same theory. This is due to the elasticity of
our concepts and the natural variations in individualistic
sensibilities, inclinations, and experience. The latter are,
however, easier to reconcile with each other. In the end,
of course, the value of any psychoanalytic proposition lies
only in the extent to which it is clinically verifiable and

useful. I have offered my discussion in the spirit that an open-minded debate of all such issues, perplexing as it sometimes may be, is nevertheless essential for the scientific growth and vitality of our profession.

DISCUSSION 4: PETER B. NEUBAUER, M.D.

Editors' Abstract

Dr. Neubauer had been invited to consider the clinical data from a developmental perspective. He regards this as an additional metapsychological point of view, one that augments those generally used by clinicians. Integrated with others, it contributes to assessing the patient's disorder and to determining ways to facilitate change. Dr. Neubauer's discussion of the clinical material is preceded by a highly condensed description of the concept of developmental processes, especially as it has evolved from the work of Anna Freud. An innovative view of how such processes influence theory and practice, it merits a careful reading. From the propositions subsumed under this point of view, Dr. Neubauer indicates how it is possible to assess features of the patterns of progression from childhood through early adulthood. These leave their residue in the final configuration of a person's psychological organization.

He suggests that Mr. A's manifest disorder of self may have been, at least partly, caused by an inherent blue print failure. This will be quite a radical view for some. Like Dr. Orgel, Dr. Neubauer considers alternatives to interpretation to assist patients in moving forward. How he applies those alternate technical activities and the theories that inform them can be usefully compared and contrasted with Dr. Orgel's positions. Careful consideration of each of their views is certain to illuminate both.

By way of informal introduction to his discussion, Dr. Neubauer commented on the very moving nature of the material presented by Dr. Lament and her efforts to grapple with it. His intention was to address selected aspects of development with particular relevance for the work with this patient. Dr. Neubauer humorously added that in his role as discussant he was lucky not to have to deal with the problems of analyst and patient who have to immerse themselves in painful affects when verbal communication is not desired. All he had to do was to speak about the developmental program.

Dr. Neubauer

It is my intention to discuss the analysis of Mr. A from the developmental point of view. To begin, I will take the liberty of making some introductory remarks about salient features of the developmental process. It seems to me there is still a lack of clarity among analysts about the role of development and maturation, in the context of both psychoanalytic theory and clinical practice. To discuss the child at any specific age does not reveal the developmental process and can only be a springboard for viewing those forces which continuously transform earlier psychic conditions. The concept of development does not refer to a specific state of mind at any specific age. It has meaning only when we refer to development as the process of change, and attempt to find the laws that govern this change: the evolvement of the inner representational world, and the emerging primacy of the reality principle over drive, wishes, and fantasies. I think we can establish the concept that the developmental change is the deepening and integration of the self.

Freud, in his "*Three Essays on the Theory of Sexuality*" (1905), introduced the perfect example of development. He outlined progressive sequences of change along with the emergence of new psychic hierarchies. Freud recognized that each new phase was discontinuous in respect to its antecedents. These libidinal phases brought together somatic needs expressed within object relationships. An overemphasis on the role of the object in understanding normal and pathological behavior fails to do justice to the influences of the other processes that affect internalization and structure formation. For example, there is an inherent pull forward toward autonomy, a pull that helps free children from their ties to the primary object and leads them toward separateness and individuation. From this point of view, Mahler's (Mahler, Pine, and Bergman, 1975) contribution is clarifying because she not only understood the powerful need for attachment but also recognized the pull forward to the ascendance toward independence. The dialogue between mother and child, their interdependency, must include Mahler's developmental steps in the process of differentiation of self and object.

Anna Freud (1965) in *Normality and Pathology of Childhood* proposes a significant new direction by declaring that progressive development is the most essential function of the immature. Therefore, it is deeply and centrally involved with the intactness or disturbance (i.e., the normality or abnormality) of this vital process. In this formulation she elevated development to one of the metapsychological dimensions.[1] Reconstruction and the genetic point of view are often mistakenly conceptualized as representing the developmental approach. According to Anna Freud, psychoanalysis depends on the analytic work that liberates those inherent forces spontaneously working in the direction of cure. From this perspective the aim of therapy is the undoing of interferences with those forces that seek normality. Thus she assumes that there are innate urges to complete development that may be assisted in therapy.

In the past, there was an expectation that the removal of unconscious conflicts, repressions, and fixations would

---

[1] It is useful to discriminate between those changes arising from the pull forward—emerging hierarchies and newly evolving organizations—from those arising from other sources such as resolution of conflicts, identification, catharsis, or the consequences of authentic subjective exchanges. The term *developmental* as a metapsychological point of view refers to the former activities, whereas in the latter, the word *development* is merely a synonym for positive changes derived from other sources.

free the ego to "do its work." This is a formulation that derives from the structural point of view. From the standpoint of developmental considerations, the elimination of fixation and repression will free those inherent forces that complete development.

I offer the proposal that such curative tendencies can be "assisted" in treatment, while still pursuing traditional aims. In the past it was asserted that any alliance with any psychic structure would violate the demand for neutrality, conceptualized as the therapist maintaining an equidistant position from all three psychic structures: id, ego, and superego. Is this also a requirement for assisting developmental progression in what Anna Freud referred to as the "immature," that is, children and adolescents? Many analysts consider the employment of technical "assistance" to be a violation of neutrality, and hence to be outside of the psychoanalytic tradition; for some, it belongs to the nonanalytic instruments of psychotherapy. It is therefore advisable to remind us that support of the ego, or of developmental progression, differs from the technique of "resolving" neurotic conflicts. Moreover, strengthening of the ego or the developmental forces will affect psychic formation. Does the inclusion of such therapeutic assistance inevitably lead to dilution, or deviation, from a more appropriate analytic intervention? I assume that developmental assistance may not only strengthen the analysis of children and adolescents, but may find some practical application in treating adults, although with certain modifications since the influence of the maturational pull forward is much more limited.

Anna Freud proposed developmental lines that result from the interaction of drive and ego–superego development, and their reaction to environmental influence, that is, between maturation, adaptation, and structuralization. Anna Freud's "developmental lines" encompass the complex interaction of the multiple factors involved in developmental progression. Anna Freud's developmental lines refer to empirical realities that inform us of the child's achievements, or his failures in development in the course of growth. Her prototype of a developmental line is that of dependency to emotional self-reliance and adult object relationships. She expected that others would fill in the details of other developmental lines, many of which were left incomplete. But, this has not as yet taken place, except in the area of early object relations.

This limitation in our knowledge recalls Hartmann's (1950) concept of multiple function of the ego apparatus, which child analysts have failed to study more thoroughly: memory, language, motility, and the like. One explanation given is that psychoanalytic technique is designed to gain access to the preconscious and unconscious, but is not equally useful for studying components of the ego apparatus, structural rather than dynamic features of the mind. Freud's early proposals of libidinal sequences were not matched by an equal knowledge of ego stages or of the maturational timetable. The psychoanalyst has to rely on other disciplines to furnish the information required to complete these lines of development. Adult clinicians feel more secure in reconstructing the past to suggest the sources of developmental interferences (such as deviation from the developmental path) than child analysts feel about predicting the result of many interlocking forces that will come into play in the future.

Does the developmental point of view inform us about therapeutic change from pathology to normality, and from fixation to progression? Our knowledge is still too limited to provide the answers to those questions. Anna Freud refers to "assimilation" and "integration" as the working through of conflicts in adults. Indeed, the psychoanalyst relies on the synthetic function and the integrative function of the ego to achieve new psychic structures. We are as yet not clear about how this process of integration or ego synthesis actually takes place. In addition, the organizational function of development does not refer to new structure formation alone. Not all changes that arise during immaturity serve development, unless changes in drive expression, superego formation, and adaptation lead to a

new organization with new hierarchies and effective transformations of the earlier developmental organization.

Fortunately, I do not have to address myself to many
of these questions, such as the role of the preverbal and
nonverbal manifestation of early development, in my response to Dr. Lament's case. However, I shall attempt to
outline the developmental profile of her patient.

It is immediately apparent that we have limited data
allowing us to outline Mr. A's developmental profile, that
is, to study the transformation of earlier conflicts to the
later stages. There is the patient's presenting problem: his
experience with Marion that profoundly evokes a feeling
of oneness and a sense of twinship with her. Mr. A could
not reexperience this feeling with Rebecca, nor with the
analyst. We hear about his longing for the mother, in spite
of what he considers to be her masculine attitude of rejecting him. We also learn that he has a similar relationship with his father, one in which he longs to be accepted
despite father's rejecting silence; here we find some evidence of his nondifferentiated object relations. There are
also some data about his adolescence—his emerging sexuality, his submissiveness to a domineering boy, his masturbation fantasies—that again reveal a difficulty in
differentiating his sexual identity, with wishes for transves-
tite behavior.

The absence of a developmental history in this case
presentation may be due to the fact that the special state of
the analysis that involves the reexperiencing of antecedent
phases has not yet clearly crystallized. However, it is also
possible that the difficulty in assessing the manifestations
of Mr. A's developmental progression is due to some basic
fault in the program, the pull or other characteristics that
inform the emergence of phases—in short, there is some
sort of developmental pathology. It is also possible that
the difficulty in assessing Mr. A's developmental progression and its manifestations is the basic pathology that char-
acterizes him and reveals a basic fault of his development.

While transformations in the course of growth are
characteristic of normality, here we appear to observe an

unchanging developmental fixation and regression with wishes for early unity with primary objects. There is the defensive wall against Mr. A's fear of nonexistence, when he is unable to satisfy his wishes for closeness to the object. This fear of his nonexistence parallels his fear of the nonexistence of the object. His resulting persistent need and longing for unity seriously compromises his ability to achieve true separateness and individuation. Mr. A's sexuality shows many features of incomplete gender differentiation. Furthermore, I do not find indications of a well-defined oedipal conflict that would be clinically evident in a struggle to love the "other," a love that contains tenderness and affection along with sexuality.

The information we have about Mr. A's adolescence does not suggest evolvement of a secondary individuation. It is of interest, in this respect, to observe his attitude toward his writing, which appears to mirror his attitude toward object relations. He wishes to lose himself in it "totally," and then responds with a writer's block. A non-differentiated, and thus a preambivalent, polarization of love and hate reflect his early psychic structure. The developmental profile reveals his basic pathology and the extent to which developmental progression was obstructed. There is the dramatic expression of the analyst's recognition that Mr. A's feelings were profoundly connected to her:

> Although I heard a small voice warning me to consider more deeply what was going on as I was able to do earlier in the hour, I now succumbed to the urgency of my feelings and I found myself blurting out, "It seems it would make you uneasy to imagine me in these terms—as though I don't see your tiredness, how low you felt in our first hour this week. Perhaps you felt I didn't understand you. As though if you were to complain to me I might lash out" (p. 15).

She further reflected,

> I felt chagrined and frustrated. Perhaps I should have left myself out of my interpretations and simply stayed with his

feelings about Rebecca, or with his dreams, I thought. In
any event, I was the one being difficult; I was the one who
wanted Mr. A to comply with my agenda due, in part, I
suppose, to my own vulnerability about being left out and
feeling forgotten [p. 15].

I understand this part of the therapy to be an expression of the patient's inability to recognize the object—most particularly the therapist or Rebecca—as
independent (outside) persons with their own feelings,
needs, and expectations of the relationship. This recognition is as yet not available to him. The analyst feels frustrated for she cannot proceed to this level of object
differentiation. She blames herself for demanding it from
him and wonders if she is embroiling herself in a contest
of wills.

There are no signs of oedipal conflicts. Although one
may observe phallic strivings, there is an absence of phallic
phase organization that would reflect itself in a greater
degree of gender differentiation. It is not surprising that
Mr. A's early psychic longings for unity interfere with expected transformations of development and maturation.
Still one ought to check whether side-by-side there may
coexist some form of developmental advance. Indeed, in
some areas this has occurred.

I am doubtful whether the change during the later
session constitutes a breakthrough, a new beginning. This
knowing about each other, patient and analyst—this expe-
riential linkage in each wished-for relationship between
mother and child—may lead to a new opening, a door to
be passed, and the condition for a move forward based on
a new dynamic constellation.

I will try to avoid the term *countertransference* in an
attempt to account for the offered data. As I reconstruct
the developmental history, the inner pain of the patient
made him turn against the primary objects, or at least
against their influence upon him, by creating a powerful
defensive wall. This colored the patient's whole attitude
toward a reality in which an individual can experience

himself as both alive and real. Can the analyst aid the patient to complete his development more effectively by establishing an alliance that facilitates that inherent pull? Winnicott might describe such a technical assist as helping a patient's creativity in the pursuit of ordinary living.

Winnicott (1958) once suggested that babies require a facilitating environment, one that among other things, permits them to overcome the tendency to compliance with caregivers by internalizing the needed objects and thereby relinquishing them. In the case of Mr. A, I suspect that he never succeeded in attaining that level of development that allowed for the relinquishing of the actual object thereby permitting true autonomy. We see a man here who is not appropriately differentiated.

Is it possible for the analyst to introduce technical measures to potentiate the residues of that inner pull toward autonomy without interfering with the basic principles of the psychoanalytic process? The patient is full of anger and criticism for not being united with his analyst. Seeing her only as a primary object is not conducive to promoting the therapeutic action that usually arises during psychoanalysis.

I don't think that we find here manifestations of deviant development, but rather interrupted development. Under such circumstances, the earliest psychic conditions fail to progress in expectable directions, possibly due to damaging influences arising from the environment. How can an analyst provide the platform from which to continue the interrupted development? Offers of assistance under such circumstances rely less on the power of reconstruction of the past than on the ability to provide a new construction. Discussing how that might be done is an undertaking better left to another time.

While I feel very comfortable with my hypotheses about Mr. A's developmental difficulties, I am also aware that a proper assessment of any patient should never be based on only one of our theoretical propositions. A full metapsychological profile is always necessary to arrive at a more balanced judgment.

EXTEMPORANEOUS REMARKS BY THE AUDIENCE AND PANELISTS

Dr. Shelley Orgel commented on the commonality between his own perspective and that of Mr. Ilahi whose emphasis upon the concept "projective identification" underlines the evocation in the analyst of affects warded off by the patient.

Dr. Lawrence Chalfin reflected on a number of specific ways in which this panel is symbolic of changes over the past fifty years. The patient presented is illustrative of the "widening scope" of cases we see. Panelists emphasize understanding not only verbal, but also nonverbal communications. There is a change from the typical earlier view of the patient's actions as primarily pathological to seeing them as communications, and recognition of the importance of embedding interpretations in an empathic context. Transference–countertransference reactions are viewed as a natural part of the work, not as pathological manifestations. A case with significant pregenital aspects might not have been selected for presentation fifty years ago. Part of being a truly modern analyst is the need to understand the past by using the transference, and being personally open to newer ways of understanding and communicating that we've come to take for granted. The integration of Loewald's work on the developmental matrix of analysis—that the transference is not just a repetition of the past but also offers a growth potential—is evident in this presentation. Dr. Chalfin also underscored that it was wonderful to have two recent graduates share their clinical work and their reflections on it.

Dr. Jules Glenn commented that Dr. Lament does a wonderful job of presenting the complexities of the analytic situation. She helps us to see the uncertainties with which an analyst struggles, and the experience of being unclear about the meanings of a patient's communications. She invites us to participate in the analysis as she did. Like the patient, he joked, he would like to hear more from her. However, unlike the patient, he will not reject what she has to say. He imagines that a lot must have gone on earlier in the analysis preparatory to the work being presented. Dr. Glenn speculated that the patient feels concern that the analyst will not appreciate him the way his father did not. Writing the novel, and not telling the analyst, must have to do with that part of his life. Both mother and father rejected him, as he feels the analyst does. Were these aspects of the earlier interpretive work? Dr. Glenn commented that, paradoxically, taking up his anger and anxiety is not meaningful unless the patient is able to trust that the analyst can work with them. That is, unless patient and analyst have actively worked with the problem of trust, such interventions will not get anywhere. Only then can effective work with the other feelings be carried out, work which is also essential to this analysis.

Dr. Leonard Shengold agreed that anger is tremendously important in this case but, putting aside theoretical differences, what comes across overwhelmingly in this analysis is the human problem: how to get to this person as a human being. He agreed with what most assume to be a tremendous step. The patient can begin to own what he feels. His problem in owning his love is as important as his anger. Whatever went on in the first few years of this analysis, Dr. Lament stayed there and lasted with the patient; she didn't die and he didn't die. This experience enables him to take that important step. The patient's silence came when he talked about his longing. It is important to help him appreciate what it means to bear this longing to his mother and his father. His only way to live in the world of both overstimulation and not getting enough was to provoke. Loving is even more terrifying, as is the coming together of both his anger and love. This way of viewing the patient's mental life, appreciating the human being that is beginning to be born, is compatible with many different theoretical approaches.

Dr. Harold Blum noted the paradoxical position he felt himself to be in; he disagreed with his usual perspective. Much
of the discussion so far has emphasized the preoedipal
aspects of the patient, a perspective with which he is typi-
cally in tune. Nevertheless in this instance he finds himself
wondering if the patient is being presented at a more
primitive level than is realistic. It is hard to imagine a
patient participating in a verbal psychoanalytic situation
who has not achieved an oedipal position. He feels that
some further attention to the issue of "otherness" is war-
ranted, particularly as it impinges on the patient's later
development, rather than seeing this as someone who
hasn't achieved separation-individuation at all.

Dr. Samuel Abrams wondered how some psychiatric residents might react to the presentation if they had wandered
into the hall. With the emphasis on despondency and emptiness, surely they would have considered the presence of
an affective disorder, probably a depression, and enter-
tained medication of one sort or another. The patient
certainly is depressed, but the analysis suggests that the
depression is informed by a profound dilemma about being too close or too far, along with the need for a sadomasochistic exchange to retain some connection. Dr. Abrams
noted that each discussant highlighted the issue of connectedness. Dr. Neubauer comments on a developmental
assist to engage the dilemma. Mr. Ilahi suggests a creative
narrative to deal with it. Dr. Lyon emphasizes the patient's
concern about being too close, lest the closeness be destructive. Dr. Abrams agreed with Dr. Orgel's impression
that we were witnessing something important happening
in the area of separateness at this juncture in the analysis.
It does require patience to create a treatable patient. Dr.
Abrams regretted that psychiatric residents were not
around so that they might be helped to recognize what
tools other than medication or short-term interventions
might be used to help someone like this get well.

Chapter 2

The Panelists Respond to One Another

EDITORS' COMMENTARY

We asked panelists to respond to one another's views of the clinical data, as presented in Chapter 1. In their initial statements, the influence of varying perspectives and different views about them were the order of the day. Our intention was to transcend the common pitfalls of the traditional panel that is primarily devoted to exchanges between the principal presenter and the discussants. Occasionally, one panelist refers to the ideas of another, but there is usually little time to reflect upon alternate positions within the panel itself. This often results in a disappointment, a sense of an opportunity missed to deeply explore and correlate differences and convergences among the participants' perspectives.

Our panelists provided a rich response. Explicitly, and often implicitly, they compared and contrasted their positions, sometimes quite sharply. They raised questions intended to clarify uncertainties, and at other times their questions assisted in discriminating issues more discretely. A careful reading of the exchange has the additional advantage of more distinctly illuminating the topic by introducing fresh data. Analysts' points of view not only inform clinical data, but also the way in which they regard the views of their colleagues. Is it possible that preferred perspectives are more than just clinical tools? Do individual panelists tend to emphasize their similarities or differences with others?

In these chapters, at least five specific questions can be tracked:

1. What forms of therapeutic action are described or implied by each participant?
2. How does each bring dynamic and structural issues together?
3. In their efforts to search out explanations, do they give greater weight to understandings of structure or of dynamics?
4. How do perspectives influence preferred techniques for dealing with the personal past? (For example, there are strikingly different views about the use of reconstruction as a technical tool. The range extends from having to be certain about accuracy in order to be effective, to asserting that reconstruction may not be correct at all and yet still remain therapeutically useful.)
5. How does each of the participants characterize his or her own orientation and the orientations of others? And, what role do characterizations such as these have in creating or sustaining the discords in our discipline?

What follows are the written responses of each panelist to the others. Some prefer a narrative form, while others direct specific comments to particular panelists.

CLAUDIA LAMENT, PH.D.

The heart of my presentation was to expose the journey that one analyst and one patient took to understanding the suffering that brought Mr. A to treatment. It was the process of how one individual arrived at the formulations of another person's internal world that I wished to show.

This included the inevitable lapses, errors, misapprehensions, and anxieties that occur and are aroused within the analyst but which, if carefully attended to, may prove invaluable to one's deeper understanding of what is taking place beneath the surface of the interactions. By implication, my hope was that some light might be thrown on the too often veiled, yet unique and highly individualized, nature of this journey for both individuals.

So then, how does one arrive at such understandings? For me, the reveries that I experienced were enormously helpful in enabling me to grasp and empathize with Mr. A's plight. These occurred in fits and starts over the course of this sequence of hours, culminating in the imagistic forms which occurred at the close of the Friday hour. Such reveries, or imaginative way stations, are means that, for me, create the possibility of a boundary crossing where one human being may feel and contemplate another's suffering—within the limits of knowing what in some sense must always remain unknowable.

In order to heighten the sense of the humanness of this journey, I chose to compose my presentation in a style devoid of psychoanalytic terminology. Yet the primitive nature of Mr. A's internal struggles was not lost on me; my dilemma was to find a means of communicating what I was discovering about him in a way that would truly reach him. For, as I realized in my early work with Mr. A, pointing out his murderousness, his view of me as a part object and other primitive fears and perceptions, did little if anything to touch him in a meaningful way. My efforts were met with open ridicule or by passive compliance, followed by mocking dismissal. To me the reason for this failure in technique was that Mr. A lacked a sense of basic trust in the other. Thus if interpretations of his primitive states and anxieties were to "hit home," his mistrust of me and others would have to be worked with, first and foremost.

To compound this issue further, Mr. A hid his profound mistrust beneath an illusory wall of oneness and merger with the other. The recognition of separateness evoked the terror of facing the mirror, of seeing himself

as alone, as apart, and as singularly responsible for all that
was inside him.

Given these problems, I also wished to demonstrate
in my presentation how one translates to the patient what
one has come to understand theoretically in a way that will
touch him emotionally. This was a most vexing problem to
tackle with Mr. A who experienced the spoken word, as
well as silences, in deeply complex ways—as recrimina-
tions, intrusions, or penetrations, to name only a few. It
is here where I find a puzzling contradiction in Mr. Ilahi's
thinking. To my mind, he has not fully considered how a
person like Mr. A—a man so mistrustful of language and
of the other, and so terrified of his separateness—could
make meaningful use of the interpretations that Mr. Ilahi
suggests should be made. To think such interpretations
would have an impact indicates that he believes Mr. A is
operating on a more highly developed level which, clearly,
Mr. Ilahi knows is not the case.

The invaluable lesson that Mr. A taught me over the
course of these hours was the power of silent contact—the
essentialness of my bearing, containing, and witnessing his
despair and hopelessness, his raging screams and silences.
When this was borne enough, then and only then could
my words have moment, to melt the isolation and, finally,
to bring down the walls.

In Dr. Neubauer's stimulating and comprehensive
discussion from a developmental viewpoint, he remarks
upon the process of introjection of the object as central
to the process of separation from the object. He also takes
up the interesting question of how one treats a man who
is not, as he put it, "appropriately differentiated. . . .
Seeing her only as a primary object is not conducive to
promoting the therapeutic action that usually arises in
analysis" (p. 65).

This astute observation brings to the fore the question
of the nature of the therapeutic action: Just how does one
proceed in this instance? I believe that both Drs. Lyon and
Orgel directly and indirectly respond to this question. In
her perceptive reactions to my work with Mr. A, Dr. Lyon

illuminated two paths. In the first she aptly notes, when I attempt to connect to Mr. A by pointing out that his view of me is based on his anxiety, he experiences this as my need to make him see me differently. This only intensifies his rage. But in the final hour of the sequence, when I connect through "an empathic acknowledgment of his state of mind" he listens and feels able to tolerate our separateness as he begins to put meaning to words. Discerningly, Dr. Lyon also recognizes another path, that of my nonverbal communication with Mr. A. In such silent messages, she speculates about the singular importance of communicating to him some sense that his rage has not harmed me, which must ease one of Mr. A's deepest anxieties. I think that in these two paths, Dr. Lyon hints at those aspects of my work with Mr. A which touch on the unorthodox notion of an analyst responding in a way that evokes the earliest mother–child connection.

In his richly evocative remarks, Dr. Orgel grasped the essence of Mr. A's predicament and directly speaks to the idea of becoming, or at least becoming like, some aspect of a patient's "primary object." It is Dr. Orgel's view that the person who can help Mr. A—a man who hears words as weapons of annihilating power—must be someone who "can submerge her identity to his when necessary; a relationship to ideas of empathy and partial temporary identification is implied" (p. 42). He stresses the importance of an analyst's being able to connect and understand silences with Mr. A, captured so beautifully in his idea of an analyst's accepting, "his needing to remain inside her, in a wordless space, until he becomes ready to move outside, into a realm where incomplete connectedness, the aloneness of otherness, prevails, and absence is imperfectly and unreliably bridged only by insubstantial words" (pp. 40–41).

Indeed, one does not ordinarily think of becoming another's "primary object" in an analytic journey, but it is increasingly my view that remnants of the earliest parent–child relationship—however transformed over time, or used for a multiplicity of purposes—do emerge within the analytic relationship. In Mr. A's case, his overwhelming need to make a sense of "oneness" with others as a protection against his aloneness in the world brings this issue into stark relief. If such yearnings are not listened to, or cast off as impossible to be worked with creatively, a treatment may go adrift or be left forever to remain in irons.

KATHLEEN LYON, M.D.

The discussions offered by Mr. Ilahi and Drs. Orgel and Neubauer are intriguing on their own, and only more so in comparison with each other. In the absence of more time to discuss the material at the conference itself, I would now like to offer a few questions and thoughts which were provoked by their comments. I find that in reviewing all the contributions the importance of words comes again to my attention. The discussants approach the clinical material from perspectives different enough that their definitions for certain words or concepts may differ. At some points they may be describing similar aspects of the patient with different words that have concordant meanings for them, perhaps appearing to disagree when they do not.

In this regard, I would have liked to know more about Dr. Neubauer's idea that Mr. A may need the analysis to provide him with a developmental assist. Would he describe any of the interventions suggested by Mr. Ilahi or Dr. Orgel as examples of interventions that would lead to such an assist? I'm not sure where, for him, analytic technique ends and "assist" begins. In his view, can a developmental assist be provided by words alone, but in a way other than interpretation, or does it pertain more to affective containment or a kind of affective being with or resonance that is gradually put into words? Dr. Neubauer refers to Winnicott in considering how to help this patient complete his development. He refers to the concept of a facilitating environment that allows the patient to internalize the object, and then separate from it. He limits his comments on this point, saying only that this assist in development should not interfere with "the basic principles of psychoanalytic process" (p. 65). This is where I would have liked to hear more.

Interestingly, Dr. Orgel seems to speak, from his perspective, to this very question. Regarding Dr. Orgel's commentary, I was particularly interested in his perspective on the patient's experience of interpretations. He feels the patient is struggling with the separateness that is a necessary prerequisite for accepting an interpretation. He quotes Poland to illustrate his point: "the negation buried in any interpretation" that "exposes and strengthens (his) essential otherness" (Poland, 2000, p. 27). He explains the patient's rejection of the analyst's comments in the Thursday session on this basis, saying, "Her interpretation comes before he has included her representation in his inner world with sufficient strength and stability for him to be able . . . to tolerate her speaking to him from outside" (p. 39). He describes the analyst's change in perspective in the next session, her feeling able to witness, rather than "deliver" the patient from his feelings, as equivalent to being able to allow the patient to remain inside her until he is ready to move outside. At this juncture words would have felt to him identical to his mother's yelling at him to "get out." In the next session, Dr. Orgel understands the patient's repetitive "no's" to be the crystallization of a new self. Separateness has become minimally bearable. I would like to know more from Dr. Orgel about how he thinks that happened. This is a mysterious moment, when self and other, word and feeling, separateness and fusion, slip back and forth. Is this patient's forward movement due to his greater ability to tolerate the pain of separation? Is this due to his feeling momentarily "internalized," not extruded, by Dr. Lament? What enables him to hold onto this experience, if this is indeed what happened?

The question of how the patient experiences interpretations is also relevant to Mr. Ilahi's comments. Mr. Ilahi, speaking from the British object relations point of view,

anticipates that his perspective may be quite divergent
from others on the panel. For myself, much of what he
had to say was relevant and credible. Without going into
a point-by-point discussion, I found his view on the aspects
of Mr. A's enactment inducing a frustrated shut out feeling
in Dr. Lament to be useful. He tells us that his way of
understanding transference and countertransference phenomena provide the analyst with access to the "more archaic and infantile parts of the patient that are beyond
words" (p. 47). He sees it as the analyst's task to decipher
the transference and countertransference, and to communicate to the patient the meaning of the exchange to the
patient. This focus leads, according to Mr. Ilahi, to very
different clinical "scenes and dialogues" (p. 48). For this
patient, in particular, I wonder how Mr. Ilahi would put
his experience into words, and how he would help the
patient with what I do feel is a very significant difficulty
with accepting and using words in the context of psychologically important relationships.

How much of the patient's difficulty in accepting the
analyst's words is thought by Mr. Ilahi to be due to the
analyst using the wrong words—offering the wrong interpretation—rather than to a more fundamental difficulty
in accepting the analyst's otherness and his own separateness? To the extent that Mr. Ilahi sees the latter as a significant issue for the patient, how would he address this?

This clinical case and the discussions that followed
seem to me to address an important and difficult area of
our work. They deal with the paradoxical dilemma of a
patient with a poorly defined sense of self who, although
he has learned to mistrust words, is struggling to put into
words feelings and fantasies that have gone unnamed up
to then. How are we to help him to find words that feel
authentic when he is so unsure of his own authenticity?
Prematurely supplying our own words and formulations
could possibly result in compliance and a continued inau-
thentic experience. I believe the only way out of the confusion is the route begun by the patient and analyst in the
presentation: slowly feeling, containing, and carefully

naming affects and the fantasies associated with them. In this way Mr. A and the analyst begin to know each other as humans who will not destroy each other in their attempt to be themselves, together yet separate.

In our original contributions all of the discussants, myself included, were grappling with whether this patient could move forward in his analysis. In my view, an im portant, if not the most important, factor in this patient's difficulties at this time is how he struggles to trust and use words. How is this difficulty to be addressed? This depends on how the difficulty is conceptualized. Is the patient experiencing a transference reenactment of his sadomasochistic relationship with his mother, or a near inability to bear the separation and negation implied by words? Or is the patient using projective identification to communicate rather than using words? Perhaps a combination of these issues is at work for him.

SHELLEY ORGEL, M.D.

Dr. Lyon beautifully, and to my ear seamlessly, derives clinical theoretical assumptions from the data she observes of this analysis. Although the words she uses to convey her hypotheses about the meanings she infers from Dr. Lament's clinical material are not mine, I found they were fully consonant with my own formulations. In a number of instances these convergences clarified or amplified my understanding of Dr. Lament's presentation. Here are just a few examples: We share the basic idea that "this patient is struggling with intense anxiety over separation and individuation" (p. 25); I also understand the patient's dream of Marion to be an expression of "a wish for the blissful fusion he imagined he experiences with her" (p. 28). Her powerful aphoristic statement that, for this patient, "the only way to be a separate individual is to be in isolation from others" (p. 31) seems exactly right. Lastly, in Dr. Lyon's reading of the resolution Dr. Lament attains on her tortuous, sometimes heartbreaking, journey through the series of sessions, she articulates our shared conclusions. She reaches a state of mind by the end of the sessions in which she feels able to tolerate and witness his great pain and despair, to simply be with and to contain his feelings.

In her paper, Dr. Lyon implicitly calls our attention to the danger of clinging to our traditional theories as a way of keeping the inner experience of the patient at a distance. Theory can be a filter, she suggests, from which emerge pictures of significantly different patients of the same analyst bearing recognizable family resemblances to each other. Theory provides an orientation in listening, using knowledge gained by study, and accumulating clinical experience to organize, integrate, and interpret manifest communications. But in addition, as Dr. Lyon shows us, loyalty to our "own" perspectives can help to avoid the wrenching away from the easier-to-bear assumptions. This is required of us if our own unguarded responses are to work as sensitive receptors to what the patient is attempting to tell us.

Dr. Lyon eloquently describes Dr. Lament's brave and fruitful struggle to approach this transparency. I also found Dr. Lament's presentation to be exciting and moving because she lets us witness the process by which she comes to realize that, in order for her to enable her patient to change, she must tolerate the relative passivity of following him—largely in silence—on what then becomes a truly shared journey.

In her reveries, Dr. Lament can imagine, through transient partial identification with Mr. A, some of the shaping subjective experiences of his childhood that are similar to, but distinct from, associated memories and fantasies derived from her own. These recollections—these juxtaposed images of her own and others' childhoods—breathe with life, reflecting a maturity and an achieved freedom from the wrappings of the developmental packages she may have inherited in her past studies at the Hampstead Clinic (now the Anna Freud Centre) and the NYU Psychoanalytic Institute.

I believe that becoming an analyst, which is the true subject of Dr. Lament's report, requires the renunciation and then reworking of the theories one has studied and incorporated, in whole or in part, in one's candidacy and for years thereafter. Such processes include the (always partial) giving up and internalization of past object relations, of core transferences to one's own analyst or analysts, to supervisors and mentors, and to the history (and mythologies) of psychoanalysis. In a sense, then, in order to meet her patient where he lives, Dr. Lament must demonstrate her belief that it is possible for a profound connectedness between two people to arise from a grief-born acceptance of their essential aloneness. One can be separate without being isolated, as Dr. Lyon says.

Mr. Ilahi's discussion begins, in contradistinction to Dr. Lyon's, with a statement that his perspective will be different from those of the other panelists, and that he will look at the clinical material from his particular orientation and viewpoint. He assumes that the other participants, brought up in a single school, one different from his, will see the patient differently. So for him theory, in essential ways, organizes what he understands of the person he is considering. Dr. Lament, Dr. Lyon, and I think our theories are rather less visible, less a tool, maybe even less an organically structured body to which we relate and through which we make interpretable order out of the ambiguities or even the confusion our patients engender. But I must wonder about the frequent phenomenon that those from what we label *other schools* seem so bound to their theories, while we believe we are so much more open to the clinical facts.

Here are a few thoughts Mr. Ilahi's paper stimulated. He comments that the patient shifted after the beginning of the analysis to teasingly inviting interpretations which he then mockingly discarded. Dr. Lament says, as Mr. Ilahi notes, that she was frustrated and puzzled for a while by this. Mr. Ilahi demonstrates how his perspective at this

point would lead him toward what was being lived out in
the transference-countertransference, and the explanations he gives are cogent. I differ from him, however, in
that I consider Dr. Lament's responses as reflections of a
potentially fertile tolerance of discomfort in not knowing,
rather than unnecessary difficulty. And I believe there was
much value to her and her patient in her numerous trial-
and-error attempts at interpreting, her steady self-reflection, and careful observation of their nonverbal, as well
as verbal, communications. In the end she comes to understandings similar to Mr. Ilahi's about what of Mr. A's childhood desperate loneliness, rage, and distrust of both his
parents was being enacted in the transference and had
filled the analytic space. And I believe she did, in her own
way, just what Mr. Ilahi says is necessary. She worked to
decipher his transference communication—verbal and
nonverbal, both inside and outside the analytic sessions—through "careful monitoring and working through
of the affects aroused in . . . her by the patient and evaluating these in the context of the rest of the patient's material" (p. 47). While she does not refer to what her patient
was doing as "very painful states . . . being desperately
evacuated" (p. 47), what she describes can be expressed
in different ways, including these. I believe that by the
end of the sequence, these states are beginning to become
thinkable, and are verbalized in the form of the patient's
repeated negations to which I have called attention in my
original presentation. What Dr. Lament reports on her
work with her patient cannot be summed up, I think, under the heading of "the more classical American ego-psy-
chological approach" (Mr. Ilahi's words, p. 48). Consider
Dr. Lament's interpretation in the third hour, for example. She describes how her patient experiences her; she
reviews her having left him alone over the weekend, char-
acterizes herself as another woman who has betrayed him,
who is sleeping, who is surrounded by great walls that will
not come down. Is she not subtly interpreting his identification of her with that part of himself derived, in turn,
from his identification with his sleeping, walled-off

mother? In the act of speaking—only when he has indicated in the preceding minutes his readiness to engage verbally with her—is she not differentiating herself from him and his representation of her? Is she indicating to him that they are indeed alone insofar as they are separate individuals, but that words taken in do restore connections with the other and can heal the splintered self?

As I write this commentary, I am impressed by how similarly Dr. Lament and the other panelists, including Mr. Ilahi, think about and do analysis at the present time. How differently those of us who began learning about analysis in the ego psychology dominated 1950s would then have approached the material we are looking at today!

But Mr. Ilahi does articulate actual differences between his orientation and those of the other panelists. I'd like to say something about one of these. Most of us also look, as he does, for allusions to the analytic situation and relationship in the patient's material, including reactions to the previous session. But, although I agree that the link to the transference is always there somewhere, I would like to think that my attention is a bit more free-floating—a bit less knowing in advance what I'll find. I don't first evaluate all associations to find a link to the analytic situation, and Dr. Lament demonstrates that she doesn't either. We have seen that she gets to understand and interpret the transference by following many nonlinear paths. I worry that regularly looking first at this particular phenomenon can skew the material toward the finding that the "immediate real concern" is the experience in the analysis. Finding anything in the analysis too regularly or labeling any one aspect the real concern troubles me. First, I find it difficult to decide that any issue is the real one, and second, patients very quickly learn what the analyst wants to hear, and will give it, or programmatically not give it. In either event, a process of analysis will have been short-circuited because the exhilarating, scary experience of surprise—which often marks and etches in memory moments when elements of the unconscious break through resistance—will have been bypassed by both analyst and analysand.

Dr. Neubauer's brief presentation of the developmental point of view shows us how his many years of study, thought, and clinical work have enabled him to achieve a refinement of concepts and questions into their deceptively simple sounding essentials. Dr. Neubauer is in basic agreement with Anna Freud's declaration "that progressive development is the most essential function of the immature." He continues: "Thus she assumes that there are innate urges to complete development that may be assisted by therapy" (p. 59). Neubauer then asks whether the analyst's assistance to developmental progression in the form, for example, of support of the ego, inevitably leads to dilution of or deviation from more appropriate analytic intervention. His position is that assisting developmental progression "may not only strengthen the analysis of children and adolescents, but may find some practical application in treating adults . . . " (p. 60).

Using Anna Freud's concept of developmental lines, Dr. Neubauer cites data from Dr. Lament's case that he will use to outline the patient's developmental profile. Once he enters into a discussion of Mr. A directly, many of his surmises and conclusions match those of the other panelists, including mine. In Dr. Neubauer's terms, Mr. A has basic developmental pathology, characterized by the wish for unity with his primary objects, a fear of nonexistence when unable to obtain closeness to the object, and a parallel fear of the nonexistence of the object. Along these same lines, for example, I noted that Mr. A experienced being silenced as an annihilation, and I described his experience of the analyst as lacking depth and dimensionality, an 'inside' in which he might seek and discover longed-for structures and capacities" (see my original discussion in chapter 1, p. 36).

Dr. Neubauer emphasizes Mr. A's inability to see objects—including the analyst—as outside, as individuals with their own subjectivities. It seems to me that this inability contributes to the analyst's doubt, during and after making interpretations, whether she should include herself in them. On the one hand, including herself would affirm her presence in the face of his attacks on her existence. On the other hand, her reference to herself as a separate subject (by the very act of interpreting) shatters his illusion (delusion?) of unity. He defensively declares she is nothing, or struggles to restore the unity by demanding silence between them. As Dr. Lament experiences a more profound understanding of herself in this relationship, including her own despairing feelings, she becomes more sensitive to the impacts on her and his inner states evoked by nonverbal contacts and communications. These include thinking in words, holding them in, speaking them, and witnessing in Poland's sense and interpretation (2000). She is able to begin to supply him with links between the nonverbal and the verbal realms, from nondifferentiation to differentiation of self and objects, from annihilating aloneness to sad loneliness, from hate to ambivalence and movement toward reparation of objects believed to be damaged or destroyed. In Mr. Ilahi's terms, she is helping him to move from the paranoid–schizoid to the depressive position. As she recognizes that her interior landscape can guide her to his, she can convey such recognition in patterns of simple words and silences that finally reach him, that express her acceptance both of the power and of the essential limitations of words.

All this, I believe, is consistent with and may represent an application of Dr. Neubauer's basic ideas about the analyst's role in aiding development. He writes in conclusion: "Offers of assistance under such circumstances rely less on the power of reconstruction of the past than on the ability to provide a new construction" (p. 65). There is evidence, I believe, in the last of her series of sessions that Dr. Lament is, indeed, creating the conditions under which developmental advance can happen for Mr. A.

M. NASIR ILAHI, L.L.M.

As I listened to and later read the interesting discussions provided by the other three panelists, it became evident to me that they and Dr. Lament significantly overlap in their overall conceptual and clinical approach. While each brings her or his own valuable specific perspective and important differences exist in their clinical understanding, their similarities become especially clear when contrasted with the line of thinking implicit or explicit in my discussion.

To understand some of the reasons for these differences one would need to step back and make a close study of our very divergent theoretical backgrounds and training. Dr. Lament and all the other panelists display a broadly American ego psychological perspective, while my own is rooted in what is loosely (and inadequately) described as British object relations theory. Such an undertaking is clearly beyond the scope of what can be achieved here. I have, therefore, confined myself to brief comments in relation to our theoretical differences during the course of my consideration of their contributions. While I am aware that these cannot do justice to our different psychoanalytic traditions, I nevertheless hope that at least some light will be shed on the otherwise perplexing and significant variations in our clinical understandings and stances.

The value of a panel such as this is that it gives us the opportunity to explore some of the real clinical implications of our theoretical differences. It enables us to more systematically examine the divergences and commonalities in our understandings than would be the case if the discussions were of a purely theoretical nature; these often become intellectualized and obscure.

Specific Comments on the Discussions of
Drs. Lyon, Neubauer, and Orgel

Drs. Orgel and Lyon both comment, in their own unique ways and in detail, on the clinical material. They also address issues of the therapeutic task faced by the analyst and of technique. However, as a number of observations that I have to make apply equally to the two of them, to avoid duplication I have chosen only to comment in some detail on the discussion by Dr. Orgel. My comments on Dr. Lyon's discussion are therefore limited to certain additional issues that she has specifically raised.

Dr. Neubauer's erudite discussion is largely, as he puts it, from a developmental perspective. For reasons of time and space, I have not entered into any detailed theoretical engagement with his views, based as they are on his elaboration from within an American ego psychological framework. As is widely known, other psychoanalytic currents also originating from Freud, such as the British independent and Kleinian schools, have formulated views on development which differ considerably in a number of respects—not only from each other, but much more significantly from all the American schools. These especially concern issues such as phases of the libido, the development of object relations, the development of the self, and the sequence of anxiety situations. The literature covering these topics is vast, and it is beyond the scope of my remarks. I have therefore confined my observations to some of the specific clinical comments Dr. Neubauer makes on Mr. A's analysis.

Dr. Orgel

Dr. Orgel's elegant discussion is both rich in clinical observations and thought provoking. At the same time there were a number of areas which I found perplexing, and which I would have liked him to clarify. There are others where it seemed that our divergence was significant. To take up all these matters in any detail so as to be able to do justice to our points of view would require much more time and space than is available here. I will therefore confine my remarks to selected aspects of his discussion.

I agree with Dr. Orgel that Mr. A "experiences as *annihilations* both his mother's attempts to silence him and his father's greeting his approaches with absent silences . . . " (p. 36). However, judging from the rest of his contribution it would appear that Dr. Orgel sees this more in relation to the older, verbal child and later adolescent in Mr. A. This is *not* the specific sense of *annihilation anxiety* associated with earliest development, as discussed by British object relations theorists. Winnicott, for example, spoke of the experience of annihilation arising from "impingement" by the early environment on infantile omnipotence which disrupts the infant's sense of "going on being." Klein linked such experience with the annihilation of the infant's ego, especially by the object within, giving rise to the ego's fragmentation and disintegration in the paranoid–schizoid position.

In Mr. A's case, I would add that he experiences mother's intrusiveness—which is the other aspect of his experience of her—as equally overwhelming and annihilating of his very being. Thus it is not so much that he installed a telephone line to prevent her from hearing "his secrets," as Dr. Orgel maintains. Rather, at a more unconscious level, these measures appear to be required as a wall against the developmentally more primitive fear of being taken over and wiped out by her.

As I point out in some detail in my original discussion, there is a great deal of evidence to suggest that he largely functions with these terrifying early anxieties and fears; the issues are much more related to others annihilating-murdering him or Mr. A doing this to his objects. All these partly conscious, but largely preconscious and unconscious, phantasies have a rather concrete quality, suggestive of their developmentally archaic origins. Moreover, this whole scenario is not only between Mr. A and his external objects but is more significantly deeply internalized. A part of him is identified with a murderous mother given to annihilating the child part, with very damaging consequences for his internal world. A failure to recognize these issues, including making clearer differentiations about the level at which he functions, will, as I note in my discussion and do so again in the remarks below, lead to significant limitations in analytic work.

Dr. Orgel states later that in the "earlier days or months it appears he could not appreciate. . . . [the analyst] . . . except as a transitional object . . . " (p. 36). I found this puzzling. An essential aspect of a transitional object situation is that the "me" and "not me" aspects are allowed to intermingle instead of being anxiously kept apart. As Winnicott points out, a great deal has to go well for the infant to be able to engage with a transitional object in a healthy way. In this view, if a patient were able to reach this stage in the transference, it would be quite a developmental achievement. Such relating is an intrinsic aspect of eventually being able to more objectively perceive objects. By contrast, Mr. A keeps things sharply apart—both inside himself and in his external relationships—a far cry from transitional object relating. His difficulty is precisely that he cannot engage in such relating. Instead, as the examples provided in my discussion indicate, he makes powerful use of projective mechanisms to evacuate unbearable mental states, making his objects the carrier of these states. One consequence of this way of functioning is that while he is able to get some immediate relief from his anxieties, he ends up being considerably damaged psychically and blocked emotionally. (In his intellectualized way he can only perceive this as a "writer's block.")

I am in full agreement with Dr. Orgel when he suggests that Dr. Lament's overinterpreting to Mr. A is also motivated by her "need to affirm . . . her *presence* . . . in the face of *his vengeful attacks on her very being* . . . " (p. 37; emphasis added). He rightly states that these are carried out in his identification with his mother. I would add that the identification is with the rejecting–annihilating part of his mother, and that in this situation the analyst is being perceived as the vulnerable child part of Mr. A that is being attacked. Dr. Orgel recognizes later that the analyst is seen as the child, but I wish to stress the importance of registering that what we are confronted with are parts of self and of objects. These are involved in projections and introjections in a complex way, as whole objects do not yet exist for Mr. A.

Thus in his opening comments, Dr. Orgel has noted Mr. A's fears both of being annihilated and of annihilating others, albeit at the level of the older child—at least so far as the transference goes. What I find perplexing is that when it comes to the detailed sessions he hardly pays attention to these issues in the transference. For instance, in his discussion of the first (Tuesday) session, like Dr. Lament he does not take up what I feel is a very illuminating weekend dream that includes within it feelings of humiliation, inadequacy, frustration, and abandonment. These represent how Mr. A tends to experience the weekend break. In his mind all this appears to be tantamount to an attack on his "very being." It is important that this be recognized in the transference, if one is not to lose empathic contact with him. While I fully agree when Dr. Orgel states that Mr. A is "imposing silence" on the analyst, to my mind this has to be understood at the level of an action on Mr. A's part. He concretely excludes the analyst now to make her the carrier of feelings he cannot bear or process, as a desperate attempt to regain his psychic balance.

This is a much more primitive level of functioning where things are experienced as presentations, rather than as representations (M. Klein's paranoid–schizoid position). Another dimension of such functioning is Mr. A's tendency to sexualization in general, and his sexuality of a frenetic quality in particular: random sexual encounters in bars, bisexual and other thoughts compulsively appearing in dreams, and so on. These are largely used unconsciously as a means of discharging bodily tension in place of consciously experiencing psychic pain and memory, as often happens with severe hysterics. Mr. A does not fit, therefore, the developmentally more integrated and relatively benign picture that Dr. Orgel appears to be implying when he states that Mr. A "achieved a version of his wish for a mirroring object . . . " (p. 37).

The sharp divergence in our respective understandings of what is transpiring in Mr. A's analysis becomes even clearer with Dr. Orgel's quotation of Poland (2000) who refers, inter alia, to the analyst being a "witness . . . who recognizes and grasps the emotional import of the patient's *self exploration* . . . " (p. 89; emphasis added). I do not see the applicability of these remarks from Poland, as the patient is engaged primarily in evacuating mental states that are split off and projected as they are *unthinkable* for him. This is a situation far removed from "self-exploration." The latter would take place if he were an ordinary neurotic with a more cohesive self. From my perspective, instead of "witnessing," the technical and therapeutic task for the analyst is twofold: first, to understand what precisely is being precariously *lived out* in this very first session of the week, and then to find suitable words to convey this understanding to Mr. A. This, to my mind, is needed to provide more genuine "holding" (Winnicott, 1958) and "containment" (Bion, 1970), so as to make it possible for some sort of integration to take place. Mr. A is not at a sufficiently advanced developmental level to permit him to experience the analyst's silence as "engaged nonintrusiveness . . . " On the contrary (as I point out in my discussion of the Wednesday and Thursday sessions), unless his anxieties are properly understood and communicated to him, prolonged silences can promote terrifying anxieties: that he has either succeeded in annihilating the analyst, or that the analyst will retaliate to annihilate him by silent attacks *in her mind.*

Dr. Orgel then skips a consideration of the Wednesday session which, as I have previously pointed out, appears to have been a very difficult one to bear for both patient and analyst. In relation to the Thursday session, I was somewhat confused by Dr. Orgel's statement that Rebecca, *in actuality,* "talked out loud" in her sleep and that she "clamors to wake him . . . *refuses* to be silent . . . " (p. 39). This does not appear to tally with Mr. A's account. While he *does* state that she attacked him with "a whole litany" (p. 13), he adds that he only remembers the words *air conditioning* and *deductions.* From the rest of his account, in which he elaborates what these two words have "previously stood for" in their quarrels, it seems to me that the "whole litany" is more likely to be what Mr. A conjured up in his own mind. Rebecca's imagined attack is always potentially available in his mind where meanings do not evolve, and words remain fixed/concrete in their old moorings. This is in contrast to the unlikely scenario that a detailed attack was delivered by a sleeping person! Dr. Orgel goes on to state that if Dr. Lament were not an analyst, she might have been provoked to do the previous day, in the silent session, what Rebecca is reported to have done to him in her sleep. No one would disagree that an analyst who verbally or otherwise attacks or retaliates against his patient has abandoned his analytic role. However (as I pointed out in my discussion), the whole point of Mr. A's communication is that he unconsciously imagines that the analyst *did* attack him in her silence ("sleep") with the same content that he attributes to Rebecca. Both financial and emotional withholding were active in the transference, when the *two of them* were silently together in the previous session.

In spite of all the analyst's good intentions and kindliness, her silence was not experienced by him as something benign, like Poland's "engaged non-intrusiveness" (Poland, 2000, p. 18), but as a dreadful attack on his "jugular." Mr. A has no idea how to symbolize the other as differentiated from the self! This is a good example of how complex and seemingly bizarre the transferences are, and how these cannot be understood without a theory about early development and early transference. Such a theory enables us to tune into the disturbances in Mr. A's capacity to symbolize, and therefore to all aspects of his verbal and nonverbal communications, including affects he arouses in the analyst. Otherwise there is a danger of collusion with what outwardly appear to be the more neurotic aspects of patients like Mr. A, without access to the underlying basic fault and archaic anxieties. It is in this area where desperate and urgent help is being sought. This situation can sometimes extend over years, even an entire analysis!

While Dr. Orgel again recognizes, in his later comments, that Mr. A's silences represent the "annihilating, silent absence[s] . . . " (p. 39) of both parents now directed at the child (now represented by the analyst), he also maintains that the analyst's interpretation "shatters an unconscious fantasy of merger . . . " (p. 39). As I have stated above, the patient's internal situation is far more complicated and persecutory. While it is true that unconsciously there is fusion between self and object, this is not a benign state and it is constantly under threat of being shattered. Neither imprecise interpretations nor remaining silent over protracted periods will help since, much to our dismay, these are not experienced as benign.

Thus if Dr. Orgel is recommending that the analyst remain a silent "witness" (which raises the question of precisely *which* aspect of this very split patient is being witnessed), it is very unclear how this will eventually "enable [Mr. A] to be a patient . . . " or to "include [the analyst's] representation in his inner world with sufficient strength and stability . . . " (p. 39). Dr. Orgel seems to suggest that words for this patient, even "the benign, careful, caring . . . " (p. 41) ones used by Dr. Lament, are tantamount to an expulsion from mother's inside. Somehow (via the conflict-free ego?) he will be able to experience her silence as a safe wordless maternal space where developmental growth will take place until he can be "delivered."

However, what this perspective does not recognize is that there is no simple polarity between words on the one hand, and silence on the other. Both are forms of symbolic communication that equally rely on the patient's capacity to symbolize experience. This is precisely the area where Mr. A and patients like him face difficulties. Until there is some restoration of this capacity, there can be no "silent witnessing" that is possible with higher functioning patients.

Therefore, I do not share the pessimism of other panelists about the use of words. There is a need for a proper recognition of Mr. A's desperate internal situation and the

splitting, denial, and projective processes at work, both
internally and in relation to the analyst. The analyst needs
to find appropriate words that will adequately convey to
the healthy part of Mr. A (noted, for instance, in my discussion of the Friday session)—which is in constant danger
of being submerged by his more destructive aspects—that
his chaotic and disowned anxieties are understood. This
is a complex task demanding a great deal from the analyst,
including a theory of early object relations and the archaic
ways in which these may be lived out. The transference
interpretations that Dr. Lament makes in the Thursday
session, while undoubtedly carefully and conscientiously
considered, are not informed by these dynamics.

It will not be surprising, therefore, that contrary to
Dr. Orgel's understanding, I do not see the first session
(Tuesday) of the following week as a "new beginning" or
"breakthrough" in the analysis. Instead, as noted in my
discussion, I believe the evidence strongly suggests increasing despair and hopelessness. From my perspective, Mr.
A's statements about his inability to sustain sexual and
loving feelings for Rebecca in particular, and to "sustain
relationships" more generally, reflect his sense of despair
that he cannot maintain his primary objects' (and, during
the weekend, his analyst's) interest in him. He seems to
attribute this to his being defective ("riddled with problems"). One is reminded of his reaction to the previous
weekend break reported in that week's first session. Now
he mentions specifically that he has had "terrible dreams"
over the weekend, including being persecuted by Nazis!
His next reference to "overpriced supermarkets," it
seems, is more a reference to his anger at having to pay
too much for the analytic food that cannot sustain him
and prevent all the terrible dreams that terrorize him. He
feels betrayed by everyone and directly expresses hopelessness that "no one," including the analyst, can help
him. While we do not have any associations to the dream
that he next reports, this seems to me to be about his
immediate transference feelings, rather than a past primal
scene phantasy being somehow autonomously recalled, as

Dr. Orgel suggests. The "writing tutor" appears to stand for the analyst whom he has approached to cure a writing block. Mr. A would like a more intellectualized tutor–student relationship with her, rather than the more terrifying emotional one!

What upsets him is his sense of betrayal, yet again over this weekend break, accompanied by paranoid feelings that his analyst will think badly about his "sexual performance." This is a further example of his frequent tendency to sexualize anything that is painful or produces anxiety. (We are reminded from the analyst's report how rejections by women are followed by sexualized dreams that, of course, also have other meanings.) Mr. A's references to his feelings about his relationship with his business colleague can, I think, be legitimately seen as his unconscious associations to this dream. Mr. A did not like this colleague's "tone of voice," and "he objected to the way [this colleague] . . . spoke to" [him]. This led to Mr. A leaving "several very angry messages" with the consequence that the colleague "withdrew . . . from me because he felt I betrayed him . . . " (p. 20).

At a deeper level, there seems to be a great deal of evidence that Mr. A believes Dr. Lament withdraws from him, not only physically but also emotionally, over the weekend. This happens because he angrily attacks her outwardly in the sessions but, more importantly, in his mind over the separations from her. Therefore, he feels he is unable to satisfy her, a feeling that he sexualizes as in the dream. We know that Mr. A is prone to seeing his close relationships as angry attacks by him, followed by the other's retaliatory attacks. This can be seen in the previous week's material. His remarks to his colleague, "C'mon! Don't you ever have arguments?" (p. 20) are really directed at the analyst. But he is convinced that this will have no impact and his fate is sealed. In other words there is a fear that the good part of his internal objects (represented by the helpful analyst) is damaged in phantasy, and cannot be repaired. This leads to real despair.

Thus contrary to what Dr. Orgel maintains, I do not see any evidence of "a new self . . . crystallizing" (p. 42). At this stage there does not appear to be a securely internalized object available to Mr. A to enable him to begin the process of separation. Dr. Lament's interpretation that links her betrayal, the weekend break, with the walled off mother does appear to provide some immediate relief from his deep despair.

However, it is interesting to see what Mr. A subsequently does with this. He first talks about feeling upset "to see yourself. You can't hide" (p. 21). But then he states, "Rebecca [who I believe stands for the analyst he is also 'living with'] has so much inside her that she doesn't see. She becomes another person at night . . . a terrorized person . . . " (p. 21). After this attack on the object he again turns his anger on himself—as he has been doing earlier in the session—regarding himself unfit for relationships and marriage, in contrast to idealized others who are "naturally" good. Mr. A's situation is existential, not "something that can be discussed or remedied . . . " (p. 21). His despair is again heavy, revealing more openly how the annihilating part of him, which attacks and breaks links with the helpful parts of the analyst over his many frustrations and separations, is now turned toward the child in himself, killing all hope. These underlying dimensions, which are actively lived out in the transference with its moment to moment shifts, have not been recognized in the analysis.

Dr. Lyon

Dr. Lyon displays sensitivity and skill in her discussion and follows the patient's material closely. However, from my perspective she, too, does not address the types of issues that I have attempted to describe in some detail in my original discussion as well as in my comments on Dr. Orgel's contribution. I will provide some brief illustrations.

Dr. Lyon correctly notes Mr. A's identification with the excluding mother and his putting the analyst in the role of "a third-party listener, listening to the talk about his novel . . . " (p. 26). But she then proceeds to offer an oedipal level explanation for this; the analyst's participation would be experienced "unconsciously as [the mother's] sexual involvement with him" (p. 26), giving rise to anxiety and guilt. Dreams of women wielding knives at his penis are seen as, "punishment for his wish to be sexual with the mother-analyst" and to place himself "in a less threatening, more passive role . . . " (p. 26). While there are some aspects of Mr. A that outwardly resemble oedipal material, a closer look suggests that his predominant anxieties concern far earlier, preverbal levels with considerable precariousness in his sense of self. There is too much complexity here, and a theoretical model involving regression in the face of oedipal conflicts is being stretched beyond its limits to accommodate all the data!

Dr. Lyon correctly observes Mr. A's inability to use defense interpretations in the first session. She links this with adolescent issues: "he experiences [such interpretations] as both an attack and a threatening seduction, undermining his attempts to see himself as a strong independent man" (p. 27). Again, while I think some adolescent themes exist superficially, the undermining he experiences is much more archaic, and at the level of his very capacity to exist as a cohesive self. This is similar to the issue noted in the previous paragraph. The fact that I have pointed this sort of theme out so often in relation both to Dr. Orgel's and Dr. Lyon's discussions underscores the enormous differences between our ways of conceptualizing, and the many clinical and therapeutic consequences of our theoretical differences.

Later, shifting to a consideration of Mr. A's relationship with his mother, Dr. Lyon offers a number of interesting thoughts in response to her question, "[What] is it like to be a child of a mother for whom you are unbearable?" (p. 30). She states, "Words are a means of asserting one's own mind, and without sanction to have one's own mind words are destroyed" (p. 31). In the rest of Dr. Lyon's discussion she, like Dr. Orgel, considers the relationship between the verbal child and the adolescent aspect of Mr. A and his mother, whereas I have drawn attention to earlier issues.

Nevertheless I would have liked her to further expand on these interesting thoughts. What does it mean when one does not have one's own mind? What types of mental functions are affected? How are words then used? What implications does all this have for subsequent development? How does this manifest itself in the clinical situation and the transference-countertransference? I believe these questions apply, with especially far-reaching implications, when we consider Mr. A's development and his relationship with his objects at a stage much earlier than what Dr. Lyon has in mind. It is patients like Mr. A who bring such questions urgently to our attention and where, from my perspective, it is difficult to make headway without engaging deeply with the areas opened up for us by the contributions of Klein, Winnicott, Bion, and many others working in these traditions.

Dr. Lyon makes some pertinent observations about defense interpretations, and how persecutory these can be for someone like Mr. A. I agree but I also pursue some additional implications of such interpretations in my earlier detailed discussion.

Dr. Neubauer

Following a succinct and clearly articulated survey of his ideas on development, Dr. Neubauer makes a number of insightful clinical observations about Mr. A's analysis. I will comment on our similarities and differences. I am in agreement with Dr. Neubauer's conclusion that there are no indications of genuine oedipal conflicts in the description we have of Mr. A. Further, his comment that Mr. A's search for unity is connected with his "seriously compromise[d] ability to achieve a true separateness and individuation . . . " (p. 63) is echoed by all the discussants.

His views are also close to mine when he observes that a "nondifferentiated, and thus a preambivalent, polarization of love and hate reveal his early psychic structure"

(p. 63). Later he states, "seeing [the analyst] only as a primary object . . . " (p. 65), implying correctly, I believe, a disturbance in Mr. A's capacity to symbolize. However, I would go further to maintain that there are unconscious phantasies, anxieties, and primitive defenses against such anxieties that are associated with these early psychic states, and that these are manifested in the treatment situation and in the transference.

I am fully aware that what I have had to say about the nature and content of these issues is not part of an American ego psychological understanding. Therefore, I have tried to detail the existence of some of these themes in my original discussion and in my remarks on Dr. Orgel's and Dr. Lyon's discussions. In contrast to Dr. Neubauer who expressly does not enter into a consideration of the therapeutic task of facilitating the patient's development from "his earliest psychic conditions" (p. 65), I have indicated that this comprises a process whereby themes such as the ones I have outlined are specifically understood and addressed. As should be quite evident by now, I do not share the view that is sometimes implicitly or explicitly put forward that preverbal anxieties and conflicts cannot be addressed in analysis.

Finally, I share Dr. Neubauer's doubts about "the change during the later session [constituting] a breakthrough, a new beginning" (p. 64), as indicated in my detailed discussion and comments on Dr. Orgel's discussion.

PETER B. NEUBAUER, M.D.

Dr. Orgel's interesting discussion leads us to understand the dynamics of the "turning point" in the road of this analysis. As I see it, he asks us to focus on the various meanings of silence between analyst and patient, and their connection with the ability to tolerate separateness, "both speaking and silent listening may express *and* create both distance and closeness, absence and penetration, hate and love" (p. 34). This significant proposition reminds us of Freud's proposal that life can be seen as a struggle between love (connectedness) and hate (disconnectedness). In a somewhat analogous fashion, Mahler's work implies that there is a continuous conflict between longing for the object and those developmental steps that move toward individuation and autonomy.

Thus, speaking and silence may express or be experienced both as closeness, oneness, and as individuation. It would be of interest to pursue this developmental line and the transformation of this conflict through the various developmental phases. Following the developmental model of the mother–child relation, we can understand Dr. Orgel's emphasis on analyst and patient becoming able to dialogue, both with silence and words. This is indeed a developmental turning point. One can only hope that it can be maintained (we have no follow-up sessions), and that the internalization of the object, with some degree of constancy, will lead to developmental reorganization.

Dr. Lyon reviews many dynamic constellations. She raises pertinent questions that, so far as we know, cannot yet be answered by the data available. From the developmental point of view, it is of interest that she emphasizes the patient's "adolescent experience": "I do think Mr. A wants her [the analyst] to go after him, but that he now experiences her as the sadistic friend, with whom issues of separation and individuation are closely bound—the adolescent elaboration of the same issues with mother" (p. 27).

Dr. Lament's account of the analytic sessions confirms the adolescent need to recreate the past, but we have, so far, insufficient evidence that the adolescent demand for reorganization to a new developmental level has been available to Mr. A. We find that early adolescents repeat preoedipal conflicts which, it is hoped, will eventually lead toward a new developmental milestone. Dr. Lyon confirms this when she states, "unable to maintain the defensive posture . . . that recreated his relationship as an adolescent, the patient regressed . . . to . . . a more . . . maternal transference" (p. 30). I assume that Dr. Lyon refers to the earliest preoedipal organization that is in some form repeated during adolescence, reexperienced but not reorganized.

Mr. Ilahi offers us a challenging view based on his alliance with British psychoanalytic propositions. While he claims differences with Dr. Lament, he nevertheless expresses views not too distant from those of the other discussants. His interpretations are based on his understanding that the clinical process is one that has its deepest layer in unconscious processes of the transference–countertransference dimension. Thus he discusses every session from this point of view, highlighting projection, denial, and splitting off. But he also explains that, "it is at a level that is beyond words and beyond his individual associations. This is a type of transference communication . . . which to my mind provides access to the more archaic and infantile parts of the patient that are beyond words" (p. 47).

This is a challenge to the psychoanalytic process. Mr. Ilahi proposes that the interaction with the analyst (particularly derived from the mother–child model) is not successful, for Mr. A's primitive anxieties have to be reached and analyzed. This can be done only by analyzing the transference. This duality in the layering of unconscious experiences deserves further discussion. How can the layers be reached in the face of the insulating wall? Does the defense have to be analyzed first, or does the object interaction between patient and analyst, silently and verbally, lead to modification of the preoedipal archaic anxieties? And how can this be brought, via transference, into the psychoanalytic process? Mr. Ilahi's formulations of the patient's internal world are important considerations for our understanding of the deep-seated roots of the patient's pathology.

Chapter 3

The Panelists Answer
Questions

EDITORS' COMMENTARY

This chapter is the final exchange between the panelists. We asked each one to respond to the specific comments, challenges, and queries about his or her perspectives, posed by the other participants. These questions had been highlighted in the letter we predistributed (see Appendix). We hoped that ambiguities would be clarified at last, and similarities and differences further articulated. Would there be a consensus about the personal perspectives that inform the panelists' clinical practice? Is it advantageous or disadvantageous that such informing structures exist?

We invite readers to judge for themselves how far panelists move from their original positions. Do they arrive at a consensus and, if so, what precisely is that consensus? We believe the panelists' well-explored arguments indicate little doubt that orientation greatly influences the way analysts find their way through the extraordinary wealth of clinical information. Free-floating attention is not so free, and does not hover so evenly in the therapeutic setting.

CLAUDIA LAMENT, PH.D.

Editors' Preface

While this chapter is principally devoted to questions the formal discussants posed to each other, Dr. Lament submitted comments as well. Responding especially to our queries she comments on the way analysts orient themselves to the patient and the process in general, and elaborates particular features of her own orientation. She goes on to explain that her preferred approach is monitoring her own responses, while tolerating the ambiguity of surfacing data. She ends by suggesting that there may very well be modes of therapeutic action that are still not clearly articulated in analytic work; too much certainty may preclude their being adequately studied.

Dr. Lament's Contribution

I was asked to comment on Mr. Ilahi's view that my work is best categorized under the rubric of "American ego psychology." My feeling about such characterizations is that however much they may be used in a shorthand way to describe someone's work, they have the effect of reducing one's efforts to a stereotype. Consequently, the analyst's hard-won attempts to break new ground—separate and apart from one's background and biases in training—evaporate in the listener's mind as he or she experiences the presentation of the analytic material. If the listener is keen to find what he thinks he should find, he will surely do so, but at a great cost; the whole enterprise of fresh listening and openness to something new will be far more likely to fall by the wayside. As many have noted, the tendency to lead with overarching theoretical ideas about who the patient is supposed to be, or how he should be feeling, is a danger in the consulting room as well.

These days I think that the rich cross-fertilization that has taken place within the British society, and actually worldwide, has infused our field with exciting challenges. Most importantly it has resulted in questioning and uncertainty in one's own preferred mode of working which is a *sine qua non* in bringing forth change. I think that the current spirit of psychoanalytic thought permits a kind of shaking up of one's comfort zone and leaves in the dust notions of "good guys versus bad guys." Several years ago, in a discussion that took up these issues, I heard Betty Joseph remark, "What I am is simply a psychoanalyst."

In the abstract I would agree with Dr. Orgel that Mr. Ilahi and I came to share similar understandings of Mr. A's childhood experiences. However, in another important way I believe that we see Mr. A very differently. That is, Mr. Ilahi thinks that from the beginning of his analysis, Mr. A was a person who could make meaningful use of the analyst's telling him directly about his primitive anxieties. I, on the other hand, do not think that Mr. A was a person who could make meaningful use of such interpretations until other matters were worked with more fully, namely, his problems with differentiation and his profound mistrust of others. These are two very different visions of Mr. A; in fact one might say that they are two entirely different people.

Second, I believe the way in which we use our countertransference reactions to understand Mr. A is quite different. For example, Mr. Ilahi read my initial reactions of puzzlement and frustration about Mr. A's material as obstacles and shortcomings in my understanding, whereas I regard and use these feelings as stepping stones toward a deeper grasp of Mr. A's communications as our work unfolds.

A question was put to me: If I do not think that my work can be easily summed up as fitting under the heading of an "ego psychological approach," how would I characterize it? At this time, I would say I am learning that with some patients—and perhaps for many—it may be the "not knowing" rather than the knowing which is of special importance for the patient's attitude and eventual movement toward change. Or posing it another way, Does the patient sense the analyst's angst in his or her own struggle to make contact? If this has happened, might it be an especially moving experience for a person such as Mr. A who has felt that the condition for love was set largely by others? I believe that helping another move toward self-discovery via one's interpretive and noninterpretive verbalizations is, most assuredly, of great help. But I also believe that other ineffables between analyst and analysand may operate in an even more powerful way. They can be difficult to pinpoint and quantify, and may be left unspoken between analyst and analysand, although they touch on the patient's central problems and vulnerabilities. Perhaps this dovetails with Dr. Neubauer's sense of the developmental turning point in the final hour of the sequence when Mr. A begins to dialogue with both silence and words.

I very much resonate with Dr. Orgel's idea that the process of becoming an analyst involves the renunciation and then reworking of one's training, including identifications with one's analyst, supervisors, and teachers. In fact, I would add that my work with Mr. A directly touches on my own difficulties around separation-individuation, and results in a reworking of these problems within myself. Actually, I think that the issue of separation arises in all my clinical work. While this is a problem that is endemic to being human, it also has personal meanings for me that arise again and again with all my patients, more with some, less with others. What I am saying is that, for me, whether it is becoming a psychoanalyst or becoming a human being, what is required is the wrenching away from and the reconciliation with my moorings.

KATHLEEN LYON, M.D.

Editors' Preface

Dr. Lyon was asked to clarify her approach, particularly in the way she viewed early mother–child difficulties and integrated them with later conflicts. She attempts to construct bridges between what appear to be widely divergent perspectives about early child development. In this bridge building she encounters difficulties. Inevitably, she returns to the question of the potential threat of theory overwhelming data as she explains her perspectives on patients owning their own minds, She concludes that too much certainty on the part of analysts may interfere with patients discovering their highly personal and individual feelings and constructions.

Dr. Lyon's Contribution

In this last round of discussions, I would like to take the opportunity to clarify some of my previous comments and respond to questions raised by the other panelists.

First, I would like to elaborate on my comment that some of Mr. Ilahi's ideas were in keeping with my own. In particular, I find both his use of dreams in the material, and his understanding of the transference interesting. For example, I agree with what he states about Mr. A who—when discussing the process of writing his novel, but not its content—is enacting in the transference-countertransference a very important piece of himself and his experience. I agree that the patient is enacting something about feeling excluded and expelled. He succeeds in eliciting needy, frustrated feelings in the analyst. However, even as I write this apparent agreement, my language diverges from that of Mr. Ilahi. I am not as comfortable with terms such as *evacuate* and *project*, although these may be very apt descriptions of the patient's mental processes. I cannot be sure from the evidence presented in the clinical material that these words best describe how this transference–countertransference constellation was produced. Mr. Ilahi's discussion of the dream of having sex with Marion, and the next dream of getting a flat tire, contains ideas that I find valuable. One example is that Mr. A's fear of being persecuted by a woman is linked to his experience of weekend breaks. Mr. Ilahi proposes that the patient attacked and murdered the absent analyst in his mind over the weekend, and fears her retribution when they are reunited. I think this sort of conceptualization of the intense and primitive rage Mr. A feels can be very useful in helping the analyst talk to patients like Mr. A.

Mr. Ilahi states that he views my contributions, as well as those of the others, as sharply different from his, in that we confine our thoughts to oedipal material. I do not see evidence for this assertion. I agree that his model of the mind affects both the language he uses and what he conceptualizes from the clinical data. This is true for every clinician. I believe my own contributions are influenced by attention to preoedipal as well as oedipal constellations. There are numerous references in my discussion to fantasies of fusion, and lack of psychological differentiation. I may not have discussed these concepts with the same language as Mr. Ilahi, or with the same model of the mind informing my comments, but I hardly confine my thinking to oedipal issues. For example, in my discussion of Mr. A's adolescent experience I utilize this material to illustrate how the analysand elaborates earlier preoedipal (sadomasochistic) conflicts in later relationships of which he has clear conscious memories. This seems useful technically, as these vivid memories potentially offer an avenue of communication between analyst and analysand about these conflicts. I certainly do not mean to imply, in referencing adolescent stage memories, that Mr. A is working from a primarily oedipal level of conflict. Instead I mean to describe his sexualization of earlier sadomasochistic, and exhibitionistic conflicts. This is how I believe Dr. Neubauer understands my comments.

Indeed, Mr. Ilahi actually acknowledges my focus on preoedipal issues in that he has asked me to elaborate on my comments about being a child whom mother experiences as unbearable, and my reflections about not having one's own words and mind. I will try to add to my thoughts on this topic. To not have one's own mind means to not have sufficient trust in the validity of one's own emotional and mental experience to be able to rely on it as an internal indicator of one's own individual mental existence. Words used to communicate one's inner experience are then drained of meaning. In this state, one must feel more vulnerable to being (and perhaps to the wish to be) affected and controlled by another person's experience and words. Exchanging words with others can then feel more like actions done to the other, or to one's self by the other. This is a more primitive state than one in which—in a defensive denial of separateness—one disavows one's own perspective and relies on, or allows oneself to be controlled by, another's perspective. I think there is some similarity between this fragile relationship to words, meaning, and mind, and what Mr. Ilahi regards as clinical manifestations of the paranoid–schizoid position.

This primitive state is more likely when early experiences of self are attacked by parental objects who cannot bear the affects and demands of a separate, yet dependent, child. The child's dependency on parental figures for everything, including the creation of meaning, requires that he comply with the parameters of the relationship that the parent creates. If the child, simply by the fact of being, is too burdensome for the parent to bear he must lessen in some way his separate existence. This results in the "soul murder" that Shengold (1989) has written about so eloquently. I think this term may apply to this patient.

I believe that if one views the mind as developing from a paranoid–schizoid position to a depressive one in infancy and very early childhood, as does Mr. Ilahi, this will affect how one sees and handles material technically. This view of development is different from that held by American ego psychologists. Mr. Ilahi repeatedly refers to feelings and fantasies for which the patient has no words. This implies that he is referring to experiences from preverbal periods. Further, he describes these mental contents as being split off, and therefore unaffected by the later developmental achievements that the patient apparently attains. In his view this results in a clinical picture in

which split-off preverbal mental contents are experienced
in the treatment through projection, enactments and
transference–countertransference constellations. It becomes, according to Mr. Ilahi, the analyst's job to put
words to these enacted mental contents.

The implications of this approach are far reaching.
It implies that the patient is unable both to analyze the
defensive reasons for splitting off this mental content and
to supply his own words. He must, therefore, rely on the
analyst to undo the defensive split and supply words. This
is very different from models that emphasize defense analysis and analyzing conflict to enable resumption of development. Rather, in Mr. Ilahi's model the interaction
between analyst and analysand seems to echo that of a
mother and very small child in which mother supplies
words to help the child begin to name his inner experience. In this situation, the analyst must be exquisitely attuned to the potential for his patient to experience aspects
of the analysis as a reenactment of the early childhood experience.

In addition, very interesting implications derive from
the idea that the analyst, like the early mother, translates
the patient's actions into words. To what extent then does
the analysand, in putting the analyst's words to his previously wordless mental content, actually or in fantasy
adopt the analyst's mental content as his own? Dr. Neubauer comments on this issue. Does the defense have to
be analyzed first, or does the object interaction between
patient and analyst, silently and verbally, lead to modification of the preoedipal archaic anxieties; and how can this
be brought via transference into the psychoanalytic
process?

All of the panelists speak, in their own ways, about
the early mother–child relationship, the identifications
with the analyst, and the analysand taking the analyst as a
primary object. Dr. Orgel, to cite one example, writes of
Dr. Lament's providing the analysand with "links between
the nonverbal and verbal realms, from nondifferentiation
to differentiation of self and objects" (p. 83). Dr. Lament

states that it is increasingly her view, "that remnants of the earliest parent–child relationship—however transformed over time, or used for a multiplicity of purposes—do emerge within the analytic relationship" (pp. 73–74).

I do not think it unorthodox to hold this view. However, as analysts we are used to relying on words. When patients have difficulty using words, or are working in areas that bring them back to preverbal experiences and mental content, we too struggle with the use of words. We must grope with our patients toward an understanding of their minds. Dr. Lament has offered us a beautiful example of just this delicate, difficult, uncertain process. Our patients entrust us with enormous responsibility. I have felt privileged to be a participant in this discussion of these profound and complex issues.

SHELLEY ORGEL, M.D.

Editors' Commentary

Dr. Orgel was asked about his ideas of therapeutic action, his concept of "levels" of psychological organization that characterized his perspective on the patient, and his view of silence as a technical instrument. He replies by describing the patient's struggle to find the optimal distance that is neither too near nor too far from the analyst, and the various ways in which this struggle goes forward. He notes that he always understands patients as functioning at many "levels" at the same time; the analyst needs to address what is functionally operative at the time. Certainty about a theory may interfere with determining which level is functionally operative at any one time. In this sense he recognizes important differences in the way he and Mr. Ilahi conceptualize the patient's disorder. Finally, Dr. Orgel further clarifies his views of the effect of silences on Mr. A.

Dr. Orgel's Contribution

In reviewing Dr. Lament's presentation and the panelists' subsequent discussions, I have realized that our focus on the few hours she reports in detail has possibly led us to underestimate the impact of the year and a half of analytic work that preceded these sessions. From Dr. Lament's summary of this period we learn that Mr. A was "serious and assiduous in setting about gaining a deeper understanding" (p. 3) of his failed love affair and his writer's block, in particular. He is described as articulate and intelligent. He is successful in his small business enterprise, and he has written at least one meritorious short story. He is capable of bringing his earlier family life and both of his parents vividly to life, and communicates penetrating observations of them that still speak feelingly of his emotional attachments and continued longings for them. He learned in the analysis how "his own approach to his own life mirrored his parents'" (p. 6).

I believe that in these first eighteen months, Mr. A became powerfully, if narcissistically, attached to his analyst. He even came to trust her stable, interested presence enough to release more primitive unconscious drives and defenses from a containment which had been made less and less secure by the intensifying erotic and aggressive aspects of his deepening transference. These currents he slowly allowed to emerge in a variety of forms, including attempts to enlist the analyst in reenacting some of these intrapsychic residues of the traumas of his early family life with his mother and father. He also spilled out a novel depicting "all this sex and aggression . . . raw and crude" (p. 8), and acted out of the transference with his new girl friend Rebecca, among other forms of externalization.

A more longitudinal focus shows us that the sessions we have been discussing occur within a long process of "descent." Mr. A could gradually allow himself to lash out at his analyst, to "absent" himself in Dr. Lament's presence, to subject her to feelings of confusion, impotent rage, helplessness, inarticulateness, and of having to accept being silenced. It was as if he exhorted: "Shut up and listen to yourself and maybe you will then hear me calling you!" The silence, his and hers, he inflicts vengefully, to be sure. But it also interposes intervals of time and space which it needs in order to be transformed into the silent witnessing that is reparative, promotes self-object differentiation, and allows reorganized ways of relating to "others."

In this sense I agree with Dr. Lyon that the series of "No's" can be thought of as creating and sustaining an emerging self in relation to a more stable object representation. We might think of the preceding "trials" Mr. A imposed (and surely there will be more just as aftershocks follow earthquakes) as his positioning himself and his analyst where and how he can tolerate their relative closeness and distance to each other. He is creating a space in which words can become deinstinctualized sufficiently to be used symbolically rather than concretely. It is at this "point" that continuing dialogue can begin (see Dr. Neubauer's earlier remarks). Much of the content he speaks is despairing, but now he can say to the analyst that he knows he cannot sustain loving and sexual feelings for Rebecca. Now, this recognition of inner conflict comes from believable self-reflection. And in this sense, too, I believe these sessions can be called a beginning of his analysis.

In her finally successful attempts to "join" him empathically—partly through her respect for his demands for silence, partly through the insights that come to her out of the filter of her reveries—she does demonstrate to him that she has temporarily internalized, rather than "extruded," him. (I agree with Dr. Lyon's comment about this.) Among other meanings, I would emphasize that Dr. Lament does offer evidence—in the course of much time and reworking—that his aggression has not "annihilated" her. Therefore, he becomes better able to tolerate separation (and separateness). He has learned, tentatively, that something of him remains in her; he is not irreparably lost to her when they are separated—by absences, by her failures to understand, by unmet wishes. I agree with those comments that stress the fragility of these new beginnings, and I see them as foundational for the difficult analytic work to follow.

I have wanted to go back to the beginning because I think doing so emphasizes that Mr. A himself, and the theory and technique applied in treating him in analysis, are not to be schematized as "either–or," all or nothing, as Mr. Ilahi seems to imply. Mr. Ilahi criticizes my discussion for addressing the patient in relation to the older, verbal child, and "*not* the specific sense of *annihilation anxiety* associated with earliest development" (p. 86). He writes that I fail to make clear "differentiations about the level at which he [Mr. A] functions " (p. 86) which, for Mr. Ilahi, has at its core "a part of him is identified with a murderous mother given to annihilating the child part, with very damaging consequences for his internal world" (p. 86). Labeling this fantasy as representing the core of Mr. A's functioning does point to very significant differences between us. An extended dialogue about these differences would be fruitful, I believe.

For now I would question (as Dr. Lament has done) how someone like Mr. A—so mistrustful of language and of the other, and so terrified of his separateness (insofar as it connotes annihilation of the child self and the needed mother)—could take in and make use of the interpretations Mr. Ilahi suggests, without the kind of work on tolerating their "being together" Dr. Lament has so movingly detailed for us. My development as an analyst had several basic principles: interpreting from the surface, addressing affective intensity and defenses against it—especially in the transference—before content, and trying to maintain an equidistant stance, in Anna Freud's sense.

I am not sure how Mr. Ilahi thinks about these classical precepts. I suspect I differ from him in degree in believing that Mr. A is an adult, an adolescent, *and* a child, including a preverbal child, in varying degrees at different times. I am not sure where Mr. Ilahi would locate the "healthy part" (p. 92) of Mr. A developmentally. But this paragraph about how he crafts interpretations suggests he and I may be in greater agreement when it comes to technical approaches than he seems to believe. I think Mr. A not only feels impelled unconsciously to destroy the child part of himself projected into the analyst, but he also holds her hand tightly as he did his mother's. He desperately needs to make sure she can hold onto him, not as tightly, as he descends, partly in the service of analysis, into the hell of his early life and infantile self. I believe he needs these evidences of her steadfastness before he can reveal to her the other more primitive levels at which he also functions. I see analysis as always moving back and forth, up, down, and sideways rather than as the more conceptually and technically unified procedure I infer Mr. Ilahi sees. For I do believe no one functions at just one level at any time, that Mr. A, in fact, never loses that part of himself which is aware of who and where he is at this point. He wants and needs the analyst to see him as complex rather than as one thing on one level.

I'll let Mr. A, in the last session, have the final word. Although I know, and I think he knows there are other levels beneath his manifest communication, coexisting with it, I believe this fragment shows convincingly what the analyst has accomplished through her necessary reflections on her confusions, missteps, and dedication to understanding herself, and therefore her patient. And Mr. A is, at these moments, capable of articulating stages of a process he has undergone on a path to insight. I believe both the process and his spoken self-observations indicate therapeutic action has occurred and will eventually be transforming. He says:

> There was that silence there, before you spoke just now, and I felt your silence greatly. Until you spoke. I felt I just spewed out all this randomness—like a catharsis on my part—but I got no insight. And I felt foolish after. And angry. Like nothing was really achieved by my speaking. It was not a catharsis, really. Like I spoke for the sake of not being silent. Like I threw out all this noise so that you could put some of this together for me.

There is self-exploration here, and a turning to the analyst, first as witness and then as interpreter. Unlike Mr. Ilahi I believe Mr. A interprets her silence here as much more "going for the jugular" (p. 52). (I refer to Mr. Ilahi's initial discussion in chapter 1.) Dr. Lament's recognizing and exploring these many meanings seem to me appropriate as a method of helping Mr. A to achieve the profound curiosity about the hidden complexities within human beings that is uniquely psychoanalytic and enables analytic change to happen.

M. NASIR ILAHI, L.L.M.

Editors' Commentary

As might have been anticipated, the other panelists posed a challenging set of questions and comments to Mr. Ilahi about his equally challenging remarks. He responds to each panelist carefully, and with extensive detail. Mr. Ilahi shares his view of the differences between his own training and what he assumes to be the training of the other participants, citing fundamental connections to Freud, Klein, and other members of the so-called British school of object relations. For example, from his perspective, the ego and defenses emerge out of the earliest mother–child interaction, rather than reflecting other autonomous derivatives. His view of mode of therapeutic action emphasizes bringing together the transference with reconstructions, thereby integrating the inferred past with the recalled past to provide an important contextual link for patients. The reader should find this very useful in putting together many of his ideas that might otherwise seem unfamiliar.

Mr. Ilahi responds to comments, stated or implied, that he may sometimes be seeing his own theories rather than the patient's productions. This strikes at the heart of the panel: How does theory inform practice? How is the optimal balance achieved? His reaction to the question is twofold. On the one hand, he says that it is important for analysts to feel their theories "in [their] bones" (p. 118). But later he adds that it is also important to wear one's theory "lightly," rather than respond to dogma, lest this interfere with being appropriately receptive to the patient and open-minded about the clinical data. It is the existence of such "images" that makes an appropriate balance so difficult to achieve.

Mr. Ilahi's Contribution

To Dr. Abrams

To the extent that all analysts today hold theories of object relations basically rooted in Freud's work, they are certainly not absent from the work of colleagues on the panel. However, my understanding of this topic takes into account some very important developments of Freud's ideas by certain contributors from the United Kingdom, especially Klein, Winnicott, and Bion. This has led to the emergence of perspectives that differ considerably from the classical views.

These British analysts have emphasized, in their different ways, that the child is very powerfully related emotionally to its objects from the earliest stages, although initially in quite an unintegrated manner. Associated with these views are also, *inter alia*, conceptualizations of the beginnings of ego formation and the nature of early defenses. While there are important differences between these British theorists on a number of issues, they nevertheless overlap significantly on the central importance of early object relations and ego formation. This is in sharp contrast to analysts rooted in the various American schools, including the classical and ego psychological ones.

From a clinical standpoint, the way one understands the nature and content of what takes place in the transference is profoundly influenced, implicitly or explicitly, by our different understandings of the areas mentioned above. The other panelists have not spelled out their views on these issues. I believe that, though there are certain broad areas of convergence between my views and theirs as a whole, a closer study will reveal the existence of some very significant differences. These include our respective understandings of the types of object relations, anxieties, and defenses that are at work in Mr. A's analysis.

The issue of the use of words and the making of interpretations is clearly a complex one with all patients, but especially so with those such as Mr. A who are at the relatively more disturbed end. Irrespective of the schools we belong to, we all have to make judgments about what and how much we interpret, and the most effective way of doing so. That almost all the other panelists have raised this issue in relation to my remarks indicates our differences in understanding what is taking place in the sessions. Implicitly or explicitly the other panelists see Mr. A as essentially a psychologically whole person, a unit, whereas I hear him mostly as deeply split. There is a healthier part that brings him into analysis and that desperately seeks life and contact with his objects, and a very destructive part in which anxieties of a psychotic nature hold sway. This latter part, which is in alliance with bad internal objects, appears to actively take over intrapsychically, and undermine the healthier bit. This promotes an atmosphere of mistrust, cynicism, and hatred in Mr. A's object relationships.

As is often the case, the relationship between these aspects of Mr. A seems to have a complex and interlocking defensive structure of an organized nature. One can hypothesize that it is the failure of this system to perform its defensive function to some degree that brings him into treatment in the first place. In my view, it is the analyst's task to help the patient recognize the nature of these issues, with particular attention to the way in which he lives them out in the transference and in his life in general. This is a complex task requiring a great deal from the analyst. He must be able to locate the different aspects of Mr. A's personality and their interrelationships—at both conscious and unconscious levels—and to find a way of communicating this understanding in words that are directed toward the healthier part of Mr. A's personality.

If these different parts of the patient are not adequately understood, and brought meaningfully together in interpretations, then it is conceivable that patients such as Mr. A can feel very judged and attacked by piecemeal interventions that address their negative aspects. These may reinforce their feeling that there is nothing of value inside them. Such reactions can, in my view, be further exacerbated and the patient further confused if interpretations of a more classical type are made that address only the defenses, without simultaneously taking account of underlying anxieties. The resulting impasses can lead to despair in both patient and analyst. It can also promote a technical view that the patient cannot bear interpretations. From this perspective all that can be offered is silent listening or an atmosphere of silent symbiotic oneness as proposed by writers such as Searles (1965), in the hope that this will calm or banish internal demons and eventually transform him into someone who is "analyzable."

While I agree that patients such as Mr. A experience the analyst's use of words as an acute reminder of their separateness from the analyst, I would extend this to include most patients. However, my own experience leads me to concur with Rosenfeld (1987) that "even patients with considerable areas of psychotic disturbance understand and value verbal communications from the analyst, when the [latter] succeeds in conveying in a precise way to the patient what he has understood. In this way the analyst's intuitive and receptive empathy is expressed in a verbal form, which has the advantage that the patient is not infantilized, i.e., not treated as if he were in fact an infant" (p. 18).

As Rosenfeld goes on to say, "this requires that the analyst fully acknowledge what the patient feels and needs but should not leave out the equally significant fact that the patient is also a separate being and an adult. It needs tact and sensitivity to interpret this to the patient so that he feels held together through the analyst's words" (p. 18).

Such interpretations that are directed toward the healthier part that can hear words, as Rosenfeld adds, are not likely to be experienced as a rejection "if the analyst's whole attitude, behavior and way of communicating also convey to the patient acceptance and understanding" (p. 18).

In relation to the point raised by Dr. Lyon, I do not believe that a patient should be supplied with anything "prematurely." Interpretations should be given, as indicated by Freud, as determined by the level of the patient's maximum unconscious anxiety (Segal, 1981). However, as I believe can be inferred from the remarks of the various panelists, the aspects of the material that we each focus on—and the meanings that we assign to them and to our own affective responses—are necessarily influenced by (amongst other factors) the psychoanalytic theories to which we subscribe in our bones. For instance, my central experience leads me to a deep belief in a whole territory of the mind, initially opened up by the contributions of the British theorists referred to earlier, that lies beneath the well-known vicissitudes of the usual Oedipus complex—which itself underlies conscious experience. Interpreting certain aspects of a patient's material from my perspective will, in turn, tend to reveal additional material that might not otherwise be reached. This will dictate new interpretations which, as Segal observes, are "seldom, if ever, used in the classical technique" (p. 3).

I concur with Dr. Lyon that authenticity is lost by premature interpretations, but would add that it is equally undermined by our not understanding, and therefore appropriately interpreting what is called for by the patient's needs.

In reference to Dr. Neubauer's point I believe, with Freud, in the importance of remembering, reconstructing, and repeating. In addition, special attention needs to be paid to acting in, or repeating in the sessions, as Joseph

(Feldman and Spillius, 1989) and a number of her colleagues have emphasized. By understanding these processes, remembering itself is fostered—not only in the sense of recalling forgotten historical events, but also making conscious object relationships, defenses, and anxieties that are unconscious. Explicitly connecting these with the patient's recounted and reconstructed past is also a crucial part of the analytic work, as it provides an important contextual link for the patient, including a sense of continuity and recognition. Precisely how such linking is accomplished is a complex issue, one outside the scope of this discussion. While the object interaction with the analyst is undoubtedly important, as stated above, its strength is critically dependent on the analyst's ability to help the patient properly understand his internal world, and thus make affective sense of his predicaments.

In relation to the point about the influence on us of our theories, this is inevitable, consciously or unconsciously. Nevertheless, I think all analysts would maintain that we should make the maximum effort to wear such theories lightly, and to view clinical data in as open-minded and emotionally receptive a manner as possible. Otherwise, instead of the analyst approaching his task without memory or desire, in Bion's terms, there will be little genuine receptiveness to the patient. Interpretations will be based more on the analyst's dogmas/preformed conceptions. Nor will there be any development in our theories, leading to deadness and stagnation. Dr. Orgel states that my views appear to be more theoretically based than his or those of Dr. Lament or Dr. Lyon—who belong to the same school. At the same time he astutely notes that this is a charge frequently made by members of a given school when they come across the views of other schools! This is an illustration of the anxieties that arise when adherents of different schools attempt to communicate with each other, especially in large conferences. I think there is a greater potential for these issues to get sorted out in small group clinical seminars that meet over an extended period of time.

How can one discern the existence of part objects in Mr. A's clinical material? It is important to note that here I am thinking not only of his relationships with anatomical part objects, but more crucially with "psychological part-objects" (Spillius, 1988). In other words, certain functions of the patient—such as capacities for judging, different types of feelings, and thinking—may be split off and, in keeping with the concept of projective identification, projected into a functional part object. I have given several examples where this appears to be happening with Mr. A. For instance, in my discussion of Dr. Lament's feeling—after the initial phase of the analysis—of being used by Mr. A as a thing, denigrated and discarded as he wished, I hypothesized that in these forms Mr. A had unconsciously split off his more unbearable needy aspects. Associated with his child part, these are projected into the analyst in such a way that the analyst is kept tantalized, frustrated, and helpless. Since this functional part of the patient is projected into a part object, Mr. A can only perceive the analyst as a "toilet" receiver of unwanted aspects of himself, and not as a whole object or person. The validity of my hypothesis is further reinforced by the numerous examples of this type of functioning that I allude to in later clinical material. If the analyst is able to discern these types of object relationships, then appropriate interventions will bring out yet additional material that will further clarify what precisely is being lived out.

How can we distinguish between the analyst's reveries and fantasies that derive from her, and those that are inserted by projections from the patient? The conceptual issues in this area have been widely elaborated and worked with in the United Kingdom for several decades, whereas they are found perplexing and are hardly ever utilized in any significant way in the United States. I share the view that a "good enough" analyst should be able—as a result of his own analysis and training—to distinguish between the aspects of his mental contents that come from his own issues and those that are affectively evoked by the patient's material, including his projections.

However, this is by no means straightforward, as it requires much discipline and skill and, in the wrong hands, can be easily misused. The analyst's own defensive needs and unconscious pulls toward collusion with the patient to evade painful issues make such introspection and self-observation unreliable, without additional corroboration from other sources such as the rest of the patient's material and the overall atmosphere of the session. I should emphasize that since many of the analyst's affective responses of this type are unconscious, and are always intertwined to some degree with the analyst's own internal issues, it may take some time for him to decipher what is taking place. With experience, the analyst internalizes to a certain extent a capacity to supervise himself, thus enabling him to make the appropriate internal differentiations. He also needs to be open to learning from his patient, which may come in the form of conscious or unconscious criticism of the analyst's interventions. There is also, of course, help that supervisors and peers can explicitly provide through consultations in difficult situations. My overall point is that internal differentiations cannot only be made, but that it is essential to do so.

If carefully used, the analyst's countertransference reactions can be a powerful source of insight into the patient's internal object relations, anxieties, and defenses, which are essentially unconscious. As previously discussed, given the preverbal nature and origin of many of these mental contents, the patient can often communicate them only by various nonverbal means, including enactments in the transference. This exerts unconscious pressure on the analyst to live out certain relationships, as has been widely discussed in the literature by a number of contemporary Kleinian and other British theorists.

Are the primitive phantasies presented to the patient creations of the analyst rather than discoveries by the patient? To the extent that all deeper analytic work relies on inferences, irrespective of the school to which the analyst may belong, this is a familiar danger inherent in psychoanalysis. However, such concerns are understandably heightened when analysts try to address the more remote forms of mental territory with their origins in infantile life, as I have attempted to do in my comments.

My understanding of the clinical material is rooted in a long clinical and theoretical orientation that has evolved in the United Kingdom. The correctness of this orientation—or of the particular way in which I have perceived Mr. A's material—is something that colleagues on the panel and readers must ponder for themselves. As a general point, those who do not subscribe to the possibility of a psychological life for the infant from the earliest stages, will find little appeal in what I have to say. Those who do allow for such a possibility will still have to deal with further major and vexing questions about the nature and content of such psychic experience. We must turn to detailed clinical reports from the analysis of adults and children that closely follow the patient's material, including responses to interventions, to find convincing clinical evidential support.

Regarding how patients get better, this involves the internalization of an internal object capable of "containing" and understanding, thus leading to a fuller understanding of the self. Corollaries are the bringing together into the central self of the previously split-off and disowned parts and impulses, especially those that are regarded as unbearably bad. This leads to a greater capacity for imaginative vitality and for distinguishing between reality and phantasy, and the development of a depressive position sense of guilt and concern for one's objects, as well as recognition of their objectivity and separateness.

To Dr. Rothstein

In relation to convergences and differences between my approach and those of other panelists, see my response to Dr. Abrams. Regarding my comment about differences between the panelists in their clinical understandings in their original discussions, an obvious example would be Dr. Orgel's perception that there was a "breakthrough" and a "new beginning" in the last session, compared to Dr. Neubauer's specific doubts about whether any such thing took place in that session.

Regarding what I meant by "perplexing," this refers largely to my specific approach to the understanding of early psychic issues and the many implications of this for technique that others have inquired about (see my response to Dr. Abrams).

Regarding the emphasis by Drs. Lyon, Neubauer, and Orgel on separation–individuation conflicts as contrasted with my understanding, we differ considerably in our views on the content of what is taking place inside Mr. A. The unconscious phantasies, types of early anxieties, defenses, and object relations that I hypothesize and that I believe can be inferred from the clinical material, are not part of the Mahler-based notions. These are more external than intrapsychic. For instance, I have noted the role of an excessive amount of splitting and projective identification whereby parts of the self and internal objects are projected into the other. This causes enormous blurring of boundaries between self and other, and significant confusion not only in this regard but in many other dimensions. Separation therefore produces unbearable anxiety.

In relation to my comment on Dr. Lyon's and Dr. Orgel's oedipal level formulations, it seems to me that this is what happens when interpretations are actually made. However, when separation–individuation issues of an earlier origin are noted, the assumption is that these cannot be dealt with at all in words.

To Dr. Orgel

Regarding differences and convergences among other panelists, I have commented on these aspects as I see them. Perhaps they have further elaborated on these in their contributions to this chapter.

Regarding the comment about the convergence between Dr. Lament's eventual understanding of the transference with mine, I agree (as I described in my initial discussion in chapter 1) that there is some similarity at the surface level. However, a closer study of my various comments, including the responses above, will show that our detailed understandings are really very different. Further, as previously discussed, I did not see any evidence to suggest that the mental states that I touched upon have become thinkable.

I agree that the analyst needs to have the capacity to experience "discomfort in not knowing" (p. 80). I would regard it as crucial for analysts to possess a capacity for creative uncertainty, or "negative capability" in the words of the poet Keats (1817). Otherwise, it would be tantamount to there being no psychic space inside the analyst where affects, ideas, and experiences are allowed to evolve and be metabolized. I was, therefore, puzzled by Dr. Orgel's observation and wondered which aspects of my comments led him to suggest this. At the same time, as I am sure Dr. Orgel would agree, the analyst's not knowing would not be a virtue in its own right.

In relation to my categorization of the position of the other panelists, I used a broad description, as it came across to me that way. I am ready to accept that this may be too restrictive and inaccurate, as such labels often are. In any event, our concern is with the substance of the different viewpoints. Here certain "alternate schools" from the United States, may well have been assimilated but I am not sure that this is true of those from across the Atlantic, such as the British independent or Kleinian orientations.

Regarding the comment about my regularly looking first at the phenomenon of transference, I recognize now that the way I worded it in my original discussion was overly schematic, and therefore capable of being misunderstood. On reflection, it seems that what led me to such a stark statement was my experience, through extensive supervision and teaching in the United States, as well as in reading Dr. Lament's otherwise elegant report. I find that transference, as I understand it, is seldom recognized or thought about by analysts in the United States, irrespective of the school to which they belong. This arises from the differences in our training to which I have previously alluded.

To highlight this, and given the time limitations of my original discussion, I made the schematic statement, which is actually a paraphrase from a paper by the British independent analyst Klauber (1981), written at an introductory level for students unfamiliar with British psychoanalysis. In actuality the analyst's listening is far more complex. Nevertheless, amongst many other factors, there is an attention to the total situation of the transference, to a "free-floating responsiveness" as a counterpart to Freud's free-floating attention (Sandler, 1976), and to the ubiquitousness of unconscious phantasy—all of which is sharply different from American conceptualizations.

By "immediate real concern" I refer to where the patient's anxieties are located at any given time. This will, of course, keep shifting from moment to moment. The analyst has constantly to be struggling to discern these anxieties, taking all aspects of the material into account, even though one may often be in the dark for extended periods of time. Nevertheless, there are moments when things come together in such a way that the analyst has a better understanding. Without the capacity to make such hypothetical distinctions, it would be difficult to keep emotional contact with the patient, to know the level, timing, and content of what we interpret—indeed do analysis at all. I therefore find it puzzling when Dr. Orgel states that he finds "it difficult to decide that any issue is the real one" (p. 81).

His next point, that "patients very quickly learn what the analyst wants to hear, and will give it, or programmatically not give it" (p. 81), is clearly something that happens if the analyst has a conscious or unconscious agenda of his own and is emotionally walled off from the patient. Clearly, no analysis can then take place. All patients learn something, consciously or unconsciously, about the way a particular analyst works, and this will have a bearing to some extent on what they bring up. But I assume that a good enough analyst will not be narcissistically blind to this, and will be able to make distinctions between authenticity and compliance.

To Dr. Lyon

I believe I have responded to the gist of Dr. Lyon's questions in my response to Dr. Abrams above.

To Dr Neubauer

I have answered Dr. Neubauer's questions in my response to Dr. Abrams and others above. I think it should be clear by now that when Dr. Neubauer refers to analyzing the transference he means something very different from my view of the concept. He, along with all the American schools, has a divergent understanding of (1) the nature and content of "transference," and (2) how this is "analyzed."

To Dr. Lament

I agree with Dr. Lament that missteps and confusions are inevitable in working with patients such as Mr. A. I would add that they exist to a greater or lesser extent with all patients, irrespective of the theories, level of experience and competence of the analyst. I have attempted to indicate my own perspective on her material. Dr. Lament's next question is about my use of words, to which I have responded in the context of Dr. Abrams's questions.

PETER B. NEUBAUER, M.D.

Editors' Commentary

Dr. Neubauer was asked if he viewed himself as principally oriented toward ego psychology. He was also asked to clarify some of his views of development. For example, could he explain the differences between level of content and level of organization? Could he further elaborate on how the need for development operates in the treatment of adults and children?

Dr. Neubauer explains that the developmental point of view is only one of the metapsychological orienting points in analysis. This point of view contributes to the study of development as a whole, while psychoanalytic treatment generally emphasizes psychic conflict. Can the developmental point of view expand the understanding of psychoanalytic treatment? Dr. Neubauer describes the interaction between environmental and inherent time table issues in the course of growth, and suggests that an assessment of the role of each in a patient's life is an important base upon which to proceed with treatment. He is prepared to consider nontransference aspects of the treatment as facilitating progress. He explains in which ways he is, and is not, an ego psychologist and ends by elaborating ways of envisioning the usefulness of developmental propositions in technique. His arguments are tightly reasoned, and his proposals so innovative that they may require a close rereading.

Dr. Neubauer's Contribution

I will address the basic questions raised about my presentation by making a few general remarks to clarify a number of points that arose during the discussion. I regard metapsychology as the conceptual framework of the theory and practice of psychoanalysis. The developmental point of view is one of the principles of metapsychology. Like all the others, it cannot stand alone as an approach for measuring the complexity of the mind. In my discussion, I intentionally limit myself to exploring the contribution of just this one frame of reference.

Development, the process of progressive change, influences all aspects of mind–brain structures and functions. Not all of those changes are equally important for psychoanalytic clinicians principally engaged in treating conflict. For example, expectable changes of the ego apparatuses—from infancy on—are less in the foreground of the customary clinical task, however significant those changes might be for a general psychoanalytic theory of development. Such changes seem less relevant when compared with the formative clinical influence of unconscious fantasy and its special demands upon the transference.

Winnicott (1958) once used the felicitous term *facilitating environment* to refer to the surround within which growth takes place. Analysts who provide developmental assistance attempt to offer an analogous facilitating environment within which the therapeutic work takes place. I believe that by understanding the complexities of psychological development analysts better position themselves to recognize the ways in which expectable conflicts arise and reside within developmental organizations. In providing a therapeutic environment that may assist in rectifying those areas of development that have gone awry, conflicts that have failed to crystallize may be able to find expression and provide a further platform for growth. This is certainly true in analyses of children and adolescents, and may be applicable to adults as well. Anna Freud's proposal of developmental lines can be an effective guide for those who wish to add the developmental perspective to their overall management of the unconscious and the transference.

This perspective facilitates assessment of the rate of change during growth, and the inherent demand for developmental completion. In assessing the potential for psychoanalysis, clinicians might wish to consider a number of features. Is the change accelerated or delayed? In which area is the expectable progression intact or vigorous? In which area is there delay? There are children whose rapid progression in one area (cognitive development, for example) may interfere with the unfolding of another area (emotional growth, for example) and thereby create specific "developmental" pathology. I think that after a period of study it is possible to determine each individual's specific style of development and to try to factor that into the therapeutic task.

In my view the patient described by Dr. Lament reveals a form of developmental arrest. His urgency to gratify needs of the earliest years, which had been inadequately fulfilled, may have interfered with overall development. It is exactly this kind of pathology which impacts upon structure, dynamics, economics; that is, on those features ordinarily subsumed under the other metapsychological points of view. What is so characteristic for this patient is the persistent powerful demand to gain from the environment a response that can finally free development to proceed along expectable lines. Regrettably, it may not be possible to provide in adult life the kind of environmental input that was necessary during infancy. It is here that the skill of the analyst is brought to bear to attempt to find paths around such arrests so that the potential for development may be reached.

Dr. Abrams's question about how to promote differentiation with a patient with such serious limitations in differentiation is a most crucial one. The answer may rely on the ability of the patient to experience basic security in the relationship with the analyst so he can find the necessary path forward, to make steps toward separateness, in Dr. Lament's case. Without sufficient differentiation between the various objects in his life, progress cannot be realized.

This, as yet, nontransference relationship with the analyst introduces a dual task: to achieve this basic acceptance or trust, and to promote the beginning of the separation of self and object. This always takes time in situations such as these, perhaps many years. Differentiation may occur earlier in some instances, for example, fantasy/reality distinctions, and later in others such as separating erotic–aggressive object relations.

This directly leads us to another proposition of the developmental point of view: the concept of developmental reorganization. There can be all kinds of useful changes within one phase. In order to achieve a truly "developmental" change, a shift to the next phase must occur. This requires the emergence of a new psychic primacy with new dynamic constellations in object-related contexts. Only when this occurs can we feel confident that earlier psychic organizations and concomitant mental representations have been replaced or abandoned by more hierarchically advanced ones.

Dr. Lament's patient does manifest adolescent aspects of functioning. However, we have no evidence that these have coalesced into a new adolescent hierarchy inclusive of object removal, expectable superego expansion, and secondary (and more definitive) individuation. This case illustrates how changes can occur within a particular phase level without the critical new "developmental" organization that is required for growth to go forward.

Dr. Orgel's reference to nonverbal power in bringing about developmental change relies on the old proposition that both preverbal and nonverbal communications are always powerful factors in psychoanalytic treatment. These are most significant when there is impairment in self-object differentiation during the first years of life. It is clear that appropriate psychoanalytic aims can only be achieved when verbal, symbolic capacities for representation can be used to explore unconscious fantasies, especially as they are represented in oedipal conflicts. I have not addressed myself to techniques for facilitating the necessary earliest differentiation, which is beyond the scope of this presentation. However, I wish to underline the seriousness of the task before us and the need to recognize that an analyst's offerings are only effective when we have overcome obstacles in the patient's ability to "take them in."

I do not agree with Mr. Ilahi's view that I am an "ego psychologist," if this implies that my primary concern is the exploration of the regulatory functions of the ego, including that of defense. Historically, the role of the ego was brought into focus because there was an overemphasis on the role of the drives. This was a step toward the widening scope of the unconscious in particular, and psychoanalytic therapy in general. Similarly, developmental considerations are neither more nor less; they add texture and nuance to dynamics and contribute to the widening scope of our profession. As I have commented earlier, I hold to the importance of integrating all metapsychological points of view to enhance psychoanalysis.

I do agree with Dr. Lament's remark that we find remnants of the earliest experiences in most patients, and with her view that without some active intervention a treatment can be derailed. This patient's massive longing to undo separateness can burden psychoanalytic goals; dealing with such longing is a necessary step to promote the psychoanalytic treatment. On the one hand these steps in the treatment process may be analogous to steps in development. At the same time I do not wish to minimize our experience that conflicts from different phases of organization can occur side by side, overlap and/or interweave. It is useful to recognize these distinctions to avoid the idea that the analytic process goes forward in a series of steps from one organization to another; for example, the fused to the autonomous, the preoedipal to the oedipal, or the oedipal back to the preoedipal. Since developmental observations demonstrate that conflicts may coexist or overlap rather than proceed in discrete steps, clinicians may be required to expand their fields of observations so as to include these realities in their work.

There were several other specific queries. In response to Dr. Lyon's inquiry, I do not adhere to a polarized view of analytic technique and developmental assistance. It is in keeping with the aims of psychoanalysis that developmental processes be recognized and given a hearing as we understand and integrate the inner life of our patient. I do accept Dr. Orgel's statement as to the need for reconstruction when there is unconscious distortion of reality. The changes that occur are the open doors that then can lead to reorganization permitting developmental progression to take place.

My discussion implies that Dr. Lament's patient has not yet achieved an oedipal developmental organization.

This does not mean that oedipal features did not inform some of his life. What it underscores is that during the oedipal period there is a new hierarchical achievement, a critical developmental change, the oedipal organization. I believe that limits in this achievement based on a variety of antecedent factors best characterize many of this patient's clinical features. Treatment is not simply to diminish the conflicts of one phase or another, but rather to understand why they did not appear in the expectable form during growth.

It is difficult to assume that there can be a true transference experience, so long as the boundaries between object and self are as blurred as we find them to be here. We see the anlage for projective identification within the analyst–patient interaction. Developmental considerations require us to differentiate transferences (the revival of past objects) from other assignments patients give to their analysts. A case like this with such early arrests is not helpful in demonstrating the various useful modalities of intervention that can be subsumed under the category of "developmental assistance." This is because the felicitous environmental input that can be thus provided is seriously compromised when the object offering it is insufficiently differentiated.

Afterword

Almost from its onset, psychoanalysis proposed one fundamental task for the analysand and another for the analyst. The patient was to "free associate;" the analyst was to attend with "freely hovering" or "free-floating" attention. The products of these activities were to provide the principal database for the growth of our enterprise.

It quickly became evident that free associations are not free. They are bound to and informed by initially unrecognized processes and complex psychological activities. If they were not so bound, they would be chaotic and unmanageable and of very little use for treatment purposes. The fact that free associations are bound leads to the principal aim of analytic work: to gain access to the unrecognized conflicts and structures that inform them. Ideas and feelings that at first seem trivial or unconnected are soon discovered to be expressions of a common coherent source such as an unconscious fantasy.

Contemporary analysts are well aware that free-floating attention is not so free either. Were it to be unbound, what analysts perceive would be equally chaotic. One function of analytic training is to contribute to an orienting base that helps to transform what is observed into something meaningful. It was originally assumed that the orienting base from which the analyst operated was inevitably concordant with the orienting base from which the patient operated. Hence, analysts could interpret apparently scattered experiences into a coherent narrative, with inevitably useful results. For example, when Freud believed that seductions caused hysteria, he readily "observed" seductions in the associations of his patients and communicated his evidence, usually with considerable conviction.

Fortunately, he was not so committed to his orientation that he could not change it whenever logic or additional empirical evidence suggested that his orienting position was either incomplete or just plain wrong. Freud's heritage is not only a body of facts and theories; it is also a willingness to recognize that the relationship between observations and hypotheses about them are in a continuing state of flux, a "work in progress" (p. 23) to use the phrase Dr. Lyon proposed in her discussion.

Hence, the topic of the panel that stimulated this volume: how hypotheses inform and misinform the way clinicians listen, and the importance of tolerating uncertainty and skepticism if a scientific endeavor is to endure. Something new defines contemporary psychoanalysis, the greater willingness of analysts to look inwards and to examine how they think, and why they think the way they do. This volume—a product of that willingness—is a useful database for all students of our discipline. The reading and rereading of each of the discussions serves to enrich our understanding of the dialectic between observer and observed.

The participants in this special study were both objective and subjective. Some may illustrate more about how they think than how they know, while others make a determined effort to be objective about their subjectivity. Several comment about the importance of tolerating ambiguity and of acknowledging that there is much that remains incomprehensible. Nevertheless, it is obvious that all recognize the necessity of having some orienting perspective within which to place their observations of their patients, and they all use these informing structures to attempt to move the process forward. Many state or at least infer that too much structure might very easily overwhelm data. While the results of applying a reified theory might be impressive, such results are the yield of faith more than science.

The patient who was studied suffered from an "optimal distance" problem in respect to his personal relationships; there were dangers of being too close or too remote. Similarly, the participants struggled with their own optimal distance problem: the dangers of being too near or too far from an orienting perspective. No one expressed this more eloquently and more excruciatingly than Mr. Ilahi when he spoke of the need to "wear such theories lightly" (p. 119) on the one hand, and to "feel it in your bones" (p. 118) on the other. It is almost impossible to integrate these images into a coherent picture. Yet that is precisely the dilemma analysts find themselves in much of the time.

Contemporary interest in different orienting perspectives, and controversies about the value of one over another, further concretize the entire problem of the necessity of a theoretical framework in order to "create" process data from observations. The proponents who engage in this struggle implicitly convey a belief that there is one genuinely real or correct unified theory that can make sense of a patient's associations to facilitate the process of cure. At the same time the challenges that arise as one "school" vies with another for supremacy only underscore the likelihood that orienting perspectives are at best heuristic devices. Perhaps it is more important for analysts to recognize how they use their own perspectives to organize the data rather than to attempt to demonstrate the superiority of these perspectives. Sometimes examining how we look at things, and why we think the way we do, may itself prove felicitous for treatment progress. At other times such reflections may allow us to recognize that our patients hear different things from what we have in mind to tell them. What could be worse for a dialogue intended for optimal communication than to have both participants walk away with the assumption that their own very different preconceived notions have been validated during the exchange? We also know that many patients benefit, at least over the short run, when they are offered and accept a reified theory that relies on faith and conviction. However, we come to recognize that, over the long run, such offerings are less valuable for them and for the growth of our discipline.

All the panelists take note of Mr. A's "boundaries" problem. However, how they account for what they see differs and, consequently, so is the way they conceptualize the nature of the therapeutic action. The contributions of each of the participants are rich. But the panel as a whole proves more valuable than the sum of its individual parts.

References

Bion, W. R. (1970), *Attention and Interpretation*. New York: Jason Aronson.

Brenner, C. (1982), *The Mind in Conflict*. Madison, CT: International Universities Press, Inc.

―――― (1994), The Mind as Conflict and Compromise Formation. *J. Clin. Psychoanal.*, 3:473–488.

Coltrera, J., Ed.,(1981), *Lives, Events, and Other Players*. New York: Jason Aronson.

Feldman, M. & Spillius, E.B., Ed. (1989), *Psychic, Equilibrium and Psychic Change: Selected Papers of Betty Joseph*. London & New York: Routledge.

Freud, A. (1965), *Normality and Pathology in Childhood*. New York: International Universities Press.

Freud, S. (1905), Three Essays on the Theory of Sexuality. *Standard Edition*, 7:123–243. London: Hogarth Press, 1953.

Hartmann, H. (1950), Comments on the Psychoanalytic Theory of the Ego. *The Psychoanalytic Study of the Child*, 7: 74–96. New York: International Universities Press.

Kanzer, M., & Glenn, J., Ed. (1979), *Freud and His Self Analysis*. New York: Jason Aronson.

―――― Glenn, J., Ed. (1980), *Freud and His Patients*. New York: Jason Aronson.

Keats, T. (1817), Letter to George and Thomas Keats, 21 December 1817. In: *Letters*, ed. M. B. Forman. London: Oxford University Press, 1952.

Klauber, J. (1981), *Difficulties in the Analytic Encounter*. New York: Jason Aronson.

Mahler, M. S., Pine, F. & Bergman, A. (1975), *The Psychological Birth of the Human Infant*. New York: Basic Books.

Orgel, S., & Fine, B. D., Ed. (1981), *Clinical Psychoanalysis*. New York: Jason Aronson.

Poland, W. S. (2000), The analyst's witnessing and otherness. *J. Amer. Psychoanal. Assn.* 48:17–34.

Reisner, S. (1999), Freud and psychoanalysis: Into the 21st century. *J. Amer. Psychoanal. Assn.*, 47:1037–1060.

Rosenfeld, H. A. (1987), *Impasse and Interpretation*. London: Routledge.

Sandler, J. (1976), Countertransference and role responsiveness. *Internat. Rev. Psychoanal.*, 3:43–47.

——— (1993), Communication from patient to analyst: Not everything is projective identification. *Internat. J. Psycho-Anal.*, 74:1097–1107.

Searles, H. (1965), *Collected Papers on Schizophrenia and Related Subjects.* London: Hogarth Press.

Segal, H. (1981), *The Work of Hanna Segal.* New York: Jason Aronson.

Shengold, L. (1989), *Soul Murder.* New Haven, CT: Yale University Press.

Spillius, E. B (1988), *Melanie Klein Today,* Vol. 1. London: Routledge.

Winnicott, D. W. (1958), *Collected Papers: Through Paediatrics to Psycho-Analysis.* London: Tavistock.

Appendix

May 18th, 2001

Dear Claudia, Kathleen, Nasir, Peter, and Shelley,

Thanks for taking the time to write your responses to the formal discussions presented at the fiftieth anniversary panel last November. We refer to these as "Round 1." As you know we are asking the five of you, once more, to respond to each other. This we call "Round 2." The endeavor as a whole seems to be turning into a short book. In a recent discussion we commented to each other that this project is developing into the kind of panel one always wishes to attend: one where there is plenty of time for discussion, and panelists thoughtfully address each others' ideas and queries.

As you work on the next "round," we'd like you to keep several things in mind. Some involve "housekeeping." Please try to confine your remarks to between six and seven double-spaced pages with approximately one-inch margins. Even though we're on a first name basis, for the purpose of publication, we'd like to standardize the more formal way of referring to the other panelists (for example, Dr. Lament, Dr. Lyon . . .). We would like to receive these contributions by July 15th.

More importantly, we wish to insure that the ideas and questions each of you raised about the work/points of view of others meet with responses. If we were still at the panel and had ample time, an alert moderator would (we hope) encourage each panelist to reply to the thoughts/challenges of the others. He or she might also highlight trends that emerge. It is in this spirit that we call each panelist's attention, individually, to ideas and queries we would like her or him to be sure to address. In addition, there are instances when one (or both of us) has a question to pose. Of course, you may feel free to include anything else you desire.

We are sending one letter to all, in the event you wish to review the issues we are flagging for each panelist's attention. We hope this is helpful and eagerly await your replies.

With very best regards,
Arden and Sam

TO CLAUDIA

From: Nasir

Do you agree with Nasir that all the other panelists (including yourself) are more similar to each other than he is to any other one, and that it is correct and "adequate" to characterize all of you as "American ego psychological"?

From: Kathleen, Nasir, Shelley

Like you, three of the four panelists take up the paradoxical issues about using words with a patient who so desperately mistrusts them. You may wish to refer to some of their specific statements to further elaborate your thinking:

Kathleen*
Nasir
Shelley

---

* Page numbers refer to each panelist's original drafts, and thus do not correspond to the pagination of this volume.

From: Shelley

Do you feel, as Shelley does (p. 5), that " in the end [you] come to understandings similar to Mr. Ilahi's about what of his (i.e., Mr. A's) childhood desperate loneliness, rage, and distrust of both his parents was being enacted in the transference and had filled the analytic space?"

Shelley states that he does not feel your work with Mr. A can be summed up under the heading "the more classical ego psychological approach" (p. 6). How would you characterize it? He also states, "becoming an analyst, which is the true subject of Dr. Lament's report, requires the renunciation and then reworking of the theories one has studied, and incorporated in whole or in part, in one's candidacy and for years thereafter . . . " (p. 3). How do you relate to this idea?

TO KATHLEEN

From: Arden

In your initial response statement, you mention that you have not undertaken "point by point" discussion of Nasir's original contribution. I, for one, would be very interested in your doing some of this. I think this would help to clarify and deepen your very interesting opening statement, "At some points they may be describing similar aspects of the patient with different words that have concordant meanings for them perhaps appearing to disagree when they do not." Do you believe that the differences between Nasir's perspective and yours, as well as the other panelists' perspectives, are as great as he believes them to be? What are the differences and convergences? Which aspects of his contribution do you already incorporate in your clinical work, find credible, etc.

From: Peter

Do you agree with his understandings of your contribution? First, that we have insufficient evidence, so far, that the patient has available the adolescent demand for reorganization to a new developmental level? Second, is he correct in assuming that you refer to the "earliest preoedipal organization that is in some form repeated during adolescence, reexperienced, but not reorganized" (p. 3)?

From: Nasir

(Since his comments are clearly stated and clustered on pages 7 and 8, they do not need much highlighting.)

He asks you, what it means clinically and theoretically to not have one's own mind?

What do you think about his view that you offer an oedipal level understanding of material that would be better conceptualized in terms of predominant anxieties deriving from earlier, preverbal levels with considerable precariousness in his sense of self? There are several statements of this idea with reference to specific content, or aspects of the analysis. Do you agree, or are you proposing (as we assume to be the case) that you attend simultaneously, and in a layered fashion, to these so-called preverbal anxieties and to anxieties associated with oedipal and adolescent development?

Would you be willing, as Nasir has requested, "to expand further on these interesting thoughts" about what it is like to be the child of a mother for whom you are unbearable (your words)? Please comment about the relationship between one's own words and differentiation from the object.

Would you comment on Nasir's thoughts about the "additional implications" of defense interpretations which, he agrees, can be experienced as persecutory for a patient such as Mr. A.

From: Shelley

He clearly loves your way of thinking and finds it compatible with and enhancing of his own. Is there anything you disagree with in his thinking, or his understanding of yours?

From: Claudia

She emphasizes your analysis of the noninterpretive elements of the analytic process that are crucial to work with Mr. A. Do you regard these as "unorthodox," as she does?

TO SHELLEY

From Sam:

Several discussants were attracted by your view of the steps taken by the patient in his establishment of separateness, in other words the nature of therapeutic action. Is it your belief that the process works by touching remnants of the earliest mother–child interaction and offering a new path for a direction that initially went awry?

From: Claudia

She addressed your remarks from the perspective of the (at least initially) noninterpretive aspects of the analytic process with Mr. A: "becoming like some aspect of [his] . . . primary object." Do you have further remarks about this?

(Kathleen asks something similar, see below.) "How do you understand the patient's being able to hold onto the experience of separateness? The 'no's' are seen as evidence of the crystallization of the self. Is it possible that the 'no's' also help create and sustain it?"

From: Kathleen

Respond to Kathleen's question (on pages 1–2 of her most recent contribution) about how it happened that the patient was able to begin to crystallize a new self, to minimally bear separateness, as evidenced in his repetitive "no's." What is your understanding of this "mysterious moment"? Kathleen asks, "Is this patient's forward movement due to his greater ability to tolerate the pain of separation? Is this due to his feeling momentarily 'internalized,' not extruded, by Claudia? What enables him to hold onto this experience, if this is indeed what happened?"

From: Nasir

He writes (p. 2 of his discussion) that, although he agrees with you that Mr. A experiences his mother's and father's silences as "annihilations," it would appear that he sees this more in relation to the older, verbal child and later adolescent in Mr. A and not in the specific sense of annihilation anxiety associated with earliest development, as discussed by British object relations theorists. Thus it is not so much that he installed a telephone line to prevent her from hearing his secrets, as Dr. Orgel maintains. Rather, at a more unconscious level, these measures appear to be required as a wall against the developmentally more primitive fear of being taken over and wiped out by her.

He adds, moreover, this whole scenario is not only between him and his external objects but, more significantly, has been deeply internalized with a part of him identified with a murderous mother given to annihilating the child part, with very damaging consequences for his internal world. A failure to recognize these issues, including making clearer differentiations about the level at which he functions, will, as I note in my discussion and do so again, in the remarks below, lead to significant limitations in analytic work. Will you comment on whether you feel this is a correct characterization of your ideas?

Nasir believes you view the patient at a "higher" level than does he. Would you have any comments about the criteria that determine levels?

Since Nasir's remarks on your discussion are voluminous (page 2 to the top of 7) and detailed, there's probably no purpose further pinpointing them. You can review them for yourself.

From: Peter

What are your thoughts about Peter's perspective on your contribution: the analyst and patient becoming able to dialogue, both with silence and words, as this relates to the developmental line of individuation and autonomy? He sees similarities to Mahler's views about separation and individuation and accepts your view that the capacity for dialogue represents a turning point. Do you see the analysis as analogous to the process of separation-individuation? How do you see that process revived or otherwise promoted in treatments such as this?

TO NASIR

You will notice a good deal of overlap among some of these comments and questions, but we thought it might be useful to detail them as they occurred.

From: Sam

Your discussion leaves the impression that you operate from an object relations perspective whereas others operate from an ego psychological perspective. Would you clarify, by citing discussions, in what ways the others so

exclusively reflect ego psychology and disregard object relations or other informing features of the mind?

Several discussants point to the issue of your use of
"words" and interpretations. Kathleen asks if it is possible
that supplying words prematurely can interfere with authenticity, and consequently with the analysis? Peter asks
if it is possible that the object interaction between analyst
and patient (both silent and verbal) can lead to modifications of the archaic relationship without reconstructions
of the presumed origins. In other words, is there something in the form of the relationship that is therapeutically
useful quite aside from words?

There are implications that your theory informs the
way you examine clinical data excessively. For example,
how is the existence of part objects discernible in the clinical material? How do you distinguish the analyst's reveries
and fantasies that derive from her own mind and past,
from those that are inserted by the projections of the patient?

You repeatedly suggest that the analyst, equipped with
a systematic theory, can see features of the clinical situation that the patient cannot see. Consequently, your interpretations in words are an attempt to convey to your
patient something that he could never discover on his
own. If this is true, how do you answer the implied question that the primitive fantasies presented to the patient
are creations of the analyst rather than discoveries by
the patient?

Finally, what is the expected mode of therapeutic action in your approach? How do your patients get better?

From: Arden

A number of the panelists (Kathleen, Shelley, Peter) state
their view that the differences between your position and
theirs are not as sharp as you seem to feel they are; that
is, they see a number of significant convergences. How do

you understand this? Do you find any common ground? It is understandable that you wish to explicate your position by examining differences. But in my opinion you might do so even more successfully if you also addressed points of agreement with other panelists. A corollary is your omission of an elaboration of what you refer to as "important differences . . . between them in their clinical understandings" in your opening statement:

Upon first listening to, and later reading, the interesting discussions provided by the other three panelists, it became evident to me that while each of them brings her or his own valuable specific perspective, and important differences exist between them in their clinical understandings, there is nevertheless a significant overlap between them and Claudia in terms of their overall conceptual and clinical approach.

In what sense do you mean "perplexing" when you write (at the end of the first paragraph of the first page of your remarks), "While I am aware that these cannot do justice to our different psychoanalytic traditions, I nevertheless hope that at least some light will be shed on the otherwise perplexing and significant variations in our clinical understandings and stances."

I was somewhat surprised to read that, in your view, Peter's discussion is based on "an American ego psychological framework." I perceive a strong influence of Anna Freud's concept of developmental lines and Margaret Mahler's separation–individuation theory. What do you think about this?

Related to this, in a number of instances (especially in relation to Kathleen's discussion) you noted your disagreement with what you construed to be oedipal formulations. At the same time, most of the panelists (Shelley, Kathleen, Peter) emphasized intense anxiety over separation–individuation conflicts. How do you see the relationships between this material and your early developmental emphasis? Is there any convergence?

On page 8 you comment, "As should be quite evident by now, I do not share the view that is sometimes implicitly or explicitly put forward that preverbal anxieties and conflicts cannot be addressed in analysis.'' Do you feel any of the other panelists maintains this position? Do you feel Peter does, since it is in the context of discussing his contribution that you make this statement?

What suggests to you (as you write on p. 8) that Shelley considers "annihilating" silences "more in relation to the older, verbal child and later adolescent in Mr. A and not in the specific sense of annihilation anxiety associated with earliest development, as discussed by British object relations theorists?''

From: Shelley

Related to my question about your considering differences among the other panelists, Shelley's comments in his "Round 1" contribution (see below) about your characterizing the other panelists (along with Claudia) as "American ego psychologists" or their technique as "the more classical ego psychological approach." He asks, is there really as much convergence among them as you ascribe to their positions? Do you see any evidence at all of disagreement amongst them?

Shelley also comments about some convergences between your ideas and those of other panelists. He feels (p. 5) Claudia came to understandings of her patient similar to yours "about what of his childhood desperate loneliness, rage and distrust of both his parents was being enacted in the transference and had filled the analytic space.'' He believes she did work to decipher the patient's transference communication, and that this began to yield results: "these states are beginning to become thinkable, and verbalized.''

Your comments have apparently conveyed the impression to Shelley that you may not frequently experience the "discomfort in not knowing" which can potentially be fertile. This is one of the points of Claudia's account of this analysis, to share with the audience this process and how she makes use of it ultimately. What do you think about this?

In a related vein, this type of clinical work, he feels, "cannot be summed up . . . under the heading of 'the more classical ego psychological approach.' " Indeed he comments, "How differently those of us who began learning about analysis in the ego psychology–dominated 1950s, would have approached the material we are looking at today!" Is this because of the assimilation of the aspects of clinical work you are highlighting, as well as assimilation of what used to be called "alternate schools?"

Are we as worlds apart as it might appear?

What are your thoughts about another of his statements?

"I worry that regularly looking first at this particular phenomenon can skew the material toward the finding that the "immediate real concern" is the experience in the analysis. Finding anything in the analysis too regularly or labeling any one aspect the real concern troubles me, first, because I find it difficult to decide that any issue is the real one, and, second, because patients very quickly learn what the analyst wants to hear, and will give it, or programmatically not give it".

From: Kathleen

Please respond to Kathleen's question (pp. 3–4).

How would you put your own countertransference experience into words for this patient, and how would you help the patient with his difficulty accepting and using words in the context of a significant relationship? Was this patient's difficulty due to the analyst using the wrong words, offering the wrong interpretations, rather than a

more fundamental difficulty accepting the analyst's otherness, and his own separateness? With regard to the latter,
how would you address this?

From: Peter

Please respond to Peter's comments (pp. 3–4) about convergences between your point of view and that of other
panelists.
   More specifically,

> while he states differences with the author, nevertheless,
> he expresses views not too distant from those of the other
> discussants. His interpretations are based on his under-
> standing that the clinical process is one which has its deepest
> layer in the unconscious process of transference–counter-
> transference dimension. . . . But, he also explains that, "It
> is at a level that is beyond words and beyond his individual
> associations and it is a type of transference communica-
> tion . . . which provides access to the more archaic and in-
> fantile parts of the patient that are beyond words."

   Peter notes,

> It [i.e., aspects of your point of view] is a challenge to
> the psychoanalytic process, for Mr. Ilahi proposes that the
> interactive part with the analyst (particularly the
> mother–child model) is not successful, for his primitive
> anxieties have to be reached and analyzed. This can only
> be done by analyzing the transference. This duality in the
> layering of unconscious experiences deserves further dis-
> cussion about how the layers can be reached in the face
> of the insulating wall.

   He asks, "Does the defense have to be analyzed first,
or does the object interaction between patient and analyst,
silently and verbally, lead to modification of the preoedipal archaic anxieties; and how can this be brought on via
transference into the psychoanalytic process?"

From: Claudia

Do you feel (as Claudia seems to imply she does) that the missteps, confusions, etc., that she describes are inevitable to working with a patient such as Mr. A? In her most recent contribution, Claudia tries to convey that a major intention of her original presentation was to convey the painful and confusing process of discovery in this analysis.

Claudia writes,

> It is here where I find a puzzling contradiction in Mr. Ilahi's thinking. To my mind, he has not fully considered how a person like Mr. A, a man so mistrustful of language and the other, and so terrified of his separateness, could make meaningful use of the interpretations that Mr. Ilahi suggests should be made. To think such interpretations would have an impact indicates that he believes Mr. A is operating on a more highly developed level, which clearly, Mr. Ilahi knows is not the case.

Can you comment on whether you see this as a contradiction, and clarify your thinking about it?

She also states that, in her view, the "silent contact" she and Mr. A had was an essential element of his being able, eventually, to find her interpretations emotionally useful. This is different from your view that she had not, up to this point, made some crucial types of interpretations.

TO PETER

From: Sam

When dealing with a patient with such a serious limitation in differentiation, what approaches do you find most helpful in promoting differentiation? (This question arises from Claudia's discussion.)

Several discussants are uncertain about your concept of reorganization, especially the suggestion that it is possible that this patient may have experienced adolescent features but without an adolescent reorganization. Can you describe differences between the features of adolescence as contrasted with the expectable reorganization of adolescence?

Almost all discussants were taken with the idea of developmental assist as a technical instrument. Can an assist occur in a form without words, for example, by assuring affective containment in the analytic setting? (from Kathleen). There are also some uncertainties as to what constitutes "developmental pathology." Shelley understands this to mean that the patient has a wish for unity with his primary objects and a fear of nonexistence for himself and others. Is developmental pathology inevitably a result of difficulties in the early mother–child dyad, or do you have some other ways of classifying developmental pathology and consequently modes of assistance?

You (and others) were characterized by Nasir as being influenced by ego psychology. Do you see yourself principally working out of an ego psychological framework?

From: Claudia

Claudia felt that your comments "bring to the fore the question of the nature of the therapeutic action: just how does one proceed in this instance?" As you put it, "the patient can only see the analyst as a primary object, a position which usually is not assigned to respond to the analytic procedure." What are your thoughts about the nature of the therapeutic action in the analysis of Mr. A?

Would you also comment about Claudia's reflection, related to a developmental perspective and undoubtedly stimulated by your remarks, as follows:

> "Indeed, one does not ordinarily think of becoming another's 'primary object' in an analytic journey, but it is

increasingly my view that remnants of the earliest parent–child relationship—however transformed over time, or used for a multiplicity of purpose—do emerge within the analytic relationship. In Mr. A's case, his overwhelming yearning for oneness as a protection against his aloneness in the world brings this issue into stark relief. If such yearnings are not listened to, or cast off as impossible to be worked with creatively, a treatment can go adrift, or left forever to remain in irons."

If you do, how does this figure into the analysis? How, if at all, do you work with this interpretively, or is it an aspect of a primarily noninterpretive mode of therapeutic action? (This point is closely related to Kathleen's second comment—see below.)

From: Kathleen

Please address Kathleen's questions to you (pages 1–2). More specifically, she asks:
    1. Would you describe any of the interventions suggested by Nasir or Shelley as examples of interventions that would lead to a developmental assist?
    2. Where does analytic technique end and "assist" begin? You state that assist in development should not interfere with "the basic principles of psychoanalytic process." Can a developmental assist be provided by words alone, but in a way other than interpretation, or does it pertain more to affective containment, or a kind of affective being with or resonance that is gradually put into words?

From: Shelley

Shelley quotes your statement, "To offer assistance in (his) development is less based on the power of reconstruction [than] on the ability to help with the construction of his

development." He then goes on to delineate some of Claudia's interventions which he construes as examples of the
analyst's role in aiding development (pp. 8–11). Do you
agree that they are, and/or do you have other thoughts
or amplifications of his perspectives to share?

From: Nasir

Nasir feels you are in agreement with him that these hours
do not represent a "turning point" in this patient's analysis. He writes (bottom of p. 8), "Finally, as my detailed
discussion as well as comments on Dr. Orgel's discussion
indicate, I share Dr. Neubauer's doubts about 'the change
during the later session [constituting] a breakthrough, a
new beginning.' " In your most recent remarks you write,
"Dr. Orgel's interesting discussion leads us to understand
the dynamics of the 'turning point' in the road of this
analysis . . . " which suggests you do feel this segment of
the analysis involves a turning point. Can you clarify what
you think about this? Do you think this is a turning point?
Or are you merely referring to Shelley's view that there
has been one?

Are you also in agreement with Nasir, as he believes
you to be, that there are no "genuine oedipal conflicts in
the description we have of Mr. A"? He states this on p. 8.

Nasir wonders how you can work without reconstructions. Don't you regard the interpretation of unconscious
phantasies, defenses, and anxieties as essential to analysis?
How can a patient get better without reconstructions?

Nasir is in basic agreement with your assessment of
the patient's developmental pathology, but adds, "I would
go further to maintain that there are unconscious phantasies, anxieties and primitive defenses against such anxiety
that are associated with these early psychic states and that
these get manifested in the treatment situation and in the
transference. . . " Do you share the view (which he believes
some analysts put forward), "implicitly or explicitly . . .

[that] preverbal anxieties and conflicts cannot be addressed in analysis''?

Do you agree with his characterization of your orientation as basically "American ego psychological"? To our ears, the work of Anna Freud and Margaret Mahler are significant influences as well.

Name Index

Subject Index